Reading and Writing about Literature

A Portable Guide

Reading and Writing about Literature

A Portable Guide

Fifth Edition

JANET E. GARDNER

JOANNE DIAZ
Illinois Wesleyan University

bedford/st.martin's
Macmillan Learning

Boston | New York

Vice President: Leasa Burton
Program Director, English: Stacey Purviance
Program Manager: John E. Sullivan III
Director of Content Development: Jane Knetzger
Executive Development Manager: Maura Shea
Assistant Editor: Cari Goldfine
Director of Media Editorial: Adam Whitehurst
Media Editor: Daniel Johnson
Executive Marketing Manager: Vivian Garcia
Marketing Assistant: Cecilia McGuinness
Senior Director, Content Management Enhancement: Tracey Kuehn
Senior Managing Editor: Michael Granger
Senior Manager of Publishing Services: Andrea Cava
Senior Content Project Manager: Lidia MacDonald-Carr
Senior Workflow Project Manager: Lisa McDowell
Production Supervisor: Robin Besofsky
Director of Design, Content Management: Diana Blume
Senior Design Manager: William Boardman
Director of Rights and Permissions: Hilary Newman
Text Permissions Researcher: Arthur Johnson, Lumina Datamatics, Inc.
Photo Permissions Editor: Angela Boehler
Director of Digital Production: Keri deManigold
Executive Media Project Manager: Michelle Camisa
Project Management: Lumina Datamatics, Inc.
Project Manager: Anandan Bommen, Lumina Datamatics, Inc.
Editorial Services: Lumina Datamatics, Inc.
Composition: Lumina Datamatics, Inc.
Cover Image: Bicho_raro/iStock/Getty Images Plus
Printing and Binding: LSC Communications

Library of Congress Control Number: 2020936679
ISBN 978-1-319-21505-7

Printed in the United States of America.
1   2   3   4   5   6   25   24   23   22   21   20

Acknowledgments

Text acknowledgments and copyrights appear at the back of the book on page 195, which constitutes an extension of the copyright page. Art acknowledgments and copyrights appear on the same page as the art selections they cover.

For information, write: Bedford/St. Martin's, 75 Arlington Street, Boston, MA 02116

Preface for Instructors

Reading and Writing about Literature: A Portable Guide, Fifth Edition, is designed to help students in literature classes master the sometimes-daunting task of writing effective critical papers. Its flexible format makes it an ideal book to be used alongside individual literary texts or any anthology lacking substantial writing instruction. It grows out of our years in the classroom working with students from diverse backgrounds and with a variety of skill levels. The text is brief and accessible enough for students to read on their own, without taking too much vital time from the central task of reading and exploring literature. It presents reading, writing, research, and critical thinking as interrelated and mutually supporting skills.

The opening chapter of this book introduces students to the value of reading literature and the unique "culture" of the literature classroom. The second chapter, on the role of good reading, shows students how to move beyond the basics of decoding and initial comprehension by emphasizing the interpretive nature of critical reading. Students are directed, through concrete examples and specific instructions, to take a more active approach to reading than many of them have taken in the past. The chapter encourages textual annotation, note-taking, journal keeping, and, above all, the crucial practice of asking questions and approaching the act of reading literature as a collaborative process between author and reader. Students should come away from this chapter more confident that their ideas and responses are a valid and necessary part of understanding literature.

The subsequent chapters devoted specifically to writing instruction further integrate critical-reading strategies as they cover the entire writing process from choosing a topic through proofreading and finalizing the formatting of the essay. Substantial attention is paid to developing an original thesis and supporting that thesis with specific evidence from the primary text as well as other sources. Separate chapters address specific issues related to thinking and writing about short fiction, poetry, and drama; students are also introduced to some of the most common sorts of writing assignments and several critical theories most useful to their examination of literary texts.

Throughout the book, critical thinking plays a central role, and nowhere is this more apparent than in Chapter 8, devoted to research. Here, the nuts and bolts of library and internet research, as well as MLA documentation, are presented in the context of true research—the sort of critical searching and synthesis that allows us to satisfy our own curiosity while contributing to the understanding of our readers. To help make these lessons more concrete to students, the book also includes a sampling of literary texts for analysis and several student papers modeling a variety of approaches and styles. Terms commonly used in literature classes appear in **boldface** throughout the text and are indexed and included in the glossary for ease of reference at the back of the book. Our hope is that this brief guide will help students increase their understanding of literature and more fully appreciate the intellectual challenges and personal rewards inherent in taking responsibility for their own responses to their reading, in their literature class and beyond.

New to the Fifth Edition

The fifth edition of *Reading and Writing about Literature* has been significantly revised and updated in the following ways:

- More streamlined explanation and instruction throughout with visual references, including new charts and examples in the coverage of: thesis, developing an argument, paraphrase and summary, explication and analysis, and understanding and avoiding plagiarism.
- Two new student essays on two new literary selections include a response paper on Zora Neale Hurston's short story "Sweat," as well as a fully documented, source-based research paper on William Butler Yeats's poem "The Second Coming."
- Updated coverage of literary criticism and theory including a new section on ecocriticism.

ACKNOWLEDGMENTS

For their helpful responses to a questionnaire about their experiences using previous editions of the book, the editors are grateful to: Jill Andert, Viterbo University; Maria Assif, University of Toronto Scarborough; Heath Diehl, Bowling Green State University; Stephen Dowell, Baptist Bible College; Paul Huebener, Athabasca University; Karlyn Koh, LaGuardia Community College/CUNY; Renee Krusemark, Northeast Community College; Paisley Mann, Langara College; Olumide Ogundipe, University of Alberta; Belinda Wheeler, Claflin University.

The editors would like to thank several individuals at Macmillan Learning, including Leasa Burton, John Sullivan, and Stacey Purviance, whose vision was instrumental in shaping the fifth edition. Thank you to our editor, Maura Shea, whose wisdom, foresight, and rigorous attention to detail made the work such a pleasure, and to our assistant editor, Cari Goldfine, for her tremendous work on preparing the manuscript. We appreciate Arthur Johnson's work in clearing permissions and Vivian Garcia and Cecilia McGuinness's marketing expertise. We especially appreciate those in production who turned the manuscript into a book: Michael Granger and Lidia MacDonald-Carr at Macmillan Learning, and Anandan Bommen at Lumina.

Joanne Diaz prepared all sections of this revised fifth edition. She thanks Brandi Reissenweber, Katy Didden, Grace Talusan, and Michael Theune for their advice on the new table of contents. She would also like to thank Megan Baker and Erin Burnison for their help with manuscript preparation.

Janet E. Gardner
Joanne Diaz

BEDFORD/ST. MARTIN'S PUTS YOU FIRST

From day one, our goal has been simple: to provide inspiring resources that are grounded in best practices for teaching reading and writing. For more than thirty-five years, Bedford/St. Martin's has partnered with the field, listening to teachers, scholars, and students about the support writers need. We are committed to helping every writing instructor make the most of our resources.

How can we help *you*?

- Our editors can align our resources to your outcomes through correlation and transition guides for your syllabus. Just ask us.
- Our sales representatives specialize in helping you find the right materials to support your course goals.
- Our learning solutions and product specialists help you make the most of the digital resources you choose for your course.
- Our *Bits* blog on the Bedford/St. Martin's English Community (**community.macmillan.com**) publishes fresh teaching ideas weekly. You'll also find easily downloadable professional resources and links to author webinars on our community site.

Contact your Bedford/St. Martin's sales representative or visit **macmillanlearning.com** to learn more.

Print and Digital Options for *Reading and Writing about Literature: A Portable Guide*

Choose the format that works best for your course, and ask about our packaging options that offer savings for students.

Print

- *Paperback.* To order the fifth edition, use ISBN 978-1-319-21505-7. To order *Reading and Writing about Literature* (print) packaged with Achieve with Gardner/Diaz, *Literature*, use ISBN 978-1-319-39434-9.

Digital

- Achieve with Gardner/Diaz, *Literature*. Achieve puts student reading, writing, and revision at the core of your course, with interactive close reading modules, a full ebook of reading and writing coverage plus an anthology of literary selections, reading comprehension quizzes, and videos of professional writers and students discussing literary works. A dedicated composition space guides students through draft, review, Source Check, reflection, and revision. For details, visit **macmillanlearning.com/college/us/englishdigital**.
- *Popular e-book formats.* For details about our e-book partners, visit **macmillanlearning.com/ebooks**.
- *Inclusive Access.* Enable every student to receive their course materials through your LMS on the first day of class. Macmillan Learning's Inclusive Access program is the easiest, most affordable way to ensure all students have access to quality educational resources. Find out more at **macmillanlearning.com/inclusiveaccess**.

Your Course, Your Way

No two literature or writing programs or classrooms are exactly alike. Our Curriculum Solutions team works with you to design custom options that provide the resources your students need. (The options below require enrollment minimums.)

- *ForeWords for English.* Customize any print resource to fit the focus of your course or program by choosing from a range of prepared topics, such as Sentence Guides for Academic Writers.
- *Macmillan Author Program (MAP).* Add excerpts or package acclaimed works from Macmillan's trade imprints to connect students with prominent authors and public conversations. A list of popular examples or academic themes is available upon request.

- *Mix and Match.* With our simplest solution, you can add up to fifty pages of curated content to your Bedford/St. Martin's text. Contact your sales representative for additional details.
- *Bedford Select.* Build your own print anthology from a database of more than eight hundred selections, or build a handbook, and add your own materials to create your ideal text. Package with any Bedford/St. Martin's text for additional savings. Visit **macmillanlearning.com/bedfordselect**.

Instructor Resources

You have a lot to do in your course. We want to make it easy for you to find the support you need—and to get it quickly.

- Instructor Resources for *Reading and Writing about Literature: A Portable Guide*, Fifth Edition, include sample syllabi and transition guides and are available as PDFs that can be downloaded from **macmillanlearning.com**.

Brief Contents

Contents

CHAPTER 1

Introduction to Reading and Writing about Literature

"Nobody reads anymore."

"People don't know how to write."

"We're becoming a nation of illiterates."

Maybe you've heard laments like these. They have sounded through our culture for several years now, indeed for at least several decades. Proclamations on the sad lack of literacy in modern life have been widely reported, as in January 2008, when Apple cofounder Steve Jobs predicted that Amazon's Kindle e-book reader was doomed to fail because "people don't read anymore." (Perhaps ironically, he said this in a room full of reporters and must have known that these writers were going to quote these words in print and that millions of people would read them.) If we take these warnings seriously, it would seem that modern culture and modern education are in big trouble.

But the news of the death of literacy is premature. In fact, we can make a good case that reading and writing occupy a more central place in our day-to-day lives than they have at any other point in history. We are bombarded all day long with written messages. Billboards, product packaging, websites, blogs, flyers, wikis, advertisements, restaurant menus, e-mails, text messages, social media updates—the list goes on and on. Even while watching TV, arguably the least literary of media, we are often given a reading task; think of the "crawl" of updates that appears at the bottom of the screen during newscasts, the captions that identify interview subjects, or even the station logos in the corner of the screen. The average North American in the early twenty-first century encounters hundreds of written messages every day, and most of us have no particular problem reading these messages. Often we don't even notice that we are doing so.

In a similar vein, most of us spend more time writing than people have at any earlier point in history. The vast majority of jobs these days require some amount of writing. Sometimes, this requirement is extensive, as when engineers write sophisticated reports on their projects, while some work-related writing is as simple as a daily e-mail to communicate with others on the job. Students, of course, take notes, complete homework assignments, and write papers. Even in our leisure time, we are likely to update our social media, comment on a friend's blog post, send a text message, or write a note to a family member or friend.

If you were to keep a list of every single thing you read and wrote in a day (a list that would, of course, have to include an entry for the list you were writing), you might be surprised at how extensive that list is by the end of the day.

So, if literacy is alive and well in the modern world, why is a book like this one necessary? Why do colleges and universities offer, or even require, literature classes? Don't we already know enough about reading and writing? Do we really need to learn how to read and write about literature? The answer as to why people *do* need to learn these skills is that imaginative literature is different from most of the other writing we read every day, and reading and writing about literature requires, and builds, a very different set of skills than those we bring to a Wikipedia article or a Facebook post.

WHY READ LITERATURE?

Let's take a moment to reflect on why we read literature. Of course, there is no single or simple answer. People read to be informed, to be entertained, to be exposed to new ideas, or to have familiar concepts reinforced. Often, people read just to enjoy a good story or to get a glimpse of how other people think and feel. But literature does much more than give us a compelling plot or a look into an author's thoughts and emotions — although at its best it does these things as well. Literature explores the larger world and the ways in which people interact with that world and with one another. So even when what we read is entirely fictional, we nevertheless learn about real life. And, indeed, by affecting our thoughts and feelings, literature can indirectly affect our actions as well. Thus literature not only reflects but even helps to shape our world.

Literature, then, is not merely informational, like so much of the reading we do in our everyday lives. It does not stand up well to haste, distractions, or multitasking. It is not meant to be browsed or skimmed as we search for particular facts or knowledge as efficiently as possible. Instead, it is designed for sustained reading, meaning that to do it justice we need to read it from beginning to end and give it our full attention for all that time. What is most important in literature is rarely highlighted for us. We must instead use our intelligence to figure out the significance the literature holds for us, and we must realize that this significance may be different for a different reader. Because of this, reading literature helps us develop the skills of introspection, sustained attention, and deep analysis, skills that can help us in other areas of our lives as well.

WHY WRITE ABOUT LITERATURE?

Even students who enjoy reading poems, stories, or plays do not always enjoy writing about them. Some claim that having to analyze literature kills the fun they find in a good story. For others, the task of writing about literature can seem intimidating, frustrating, or just plain dull. If you share any of these prejudices, try to put them aside while we consider the value of writing about literature.

Writing about literature requires a special set of knowledge and skills. When you write about a story, a poem, or a play, you need to be particularly attentive to language, the medium of literature. This hones both analytical ability and creativity. In this sort of writing, you also need to pay close attention to your own use of language—just as you must pay attention to the language of the story, poem, or play—and doing so may have ripple effects that improve all your writing. Writing about literature, then, can help make you more thoughtful and articulate, better able to make yourself heard and understood, and obviously those are qualities that can improve your life well beyond the bounds of your literature classroom. And, far from killing the enjoyment of reading, writing about literature can increase that enjoyment and provide a sense of accomplishment as you look at the well-crafted paper that you've written.

Writing about literature also helps in the real world. By forcing us to organize our thoughts and state clearly what we think, writing an essay helps us clarify what we know and believe. It gives us a chance to affect the thinking of our readers. Even more important, we actually learn as we write. In the process of writing, we often make new discoveries and forge new connections between ideas. We find and work through contradictions in our thinking, and we create whole new lines of thought as we work to make linear sense out of an often chaotic jumble of impressions. So, while *reading* literature can teach us much about the world, *writing* about literature often teaches us about ourselves.

WHAT TO EXPECT IN A LITERATURE CLASS

Every classroom, like every group of people in any setting, is its own unique world, with its own set of expectations and social interactions. However, there are certain features common to most literature classes, what might be considered the culture of a college or university literature class.

Unlike some other classes on campus, a literature class is not the sort of class in which attendance is optional as long as you master the material and are able to pass the tests. Though your class may have a lecture component, it will almost certainly have a large discussion component as well, a give-and-take between students and instructor regarding the stories, poems, and plays you have read. In some ways, these discussions are the most important part of a literature class, and no amount of extra study on your own or sharing notes with a classmate can make up for having missed class. To follow these discussions, let alone to participate, you obviously will have to complete the reading. Whether or not your class has a stated attendance policy, to do well you need to be there and to be caught up with all reading and writing assignments—participation is important.

Discussions in literature classes are usually interesting because no two people come away from a particular literary text with exactly the same impressions. You may dislike a particular story and be surprised to discover that most of your fellow students loved it. A poem may leave you smiling while it makes one of your classmates cry. A character's motivation might seem obvious to you but baffle someone else. These differences arise because each reader is distinctive. Because you have lived a unique life, you have a knowledge of the world that is slightly different from any other reader's. You bring this personal history and knowledge to your reading, along with your own mind and temperament, your own likes and dislikes, and even all the knowledge gained from your past reading. Differing opinions are valid in literature classes, and each reader is in a position to enrich the conversation by speaking up in class.

Just as speaking up is part of participating, so, too, is attentive listening. While it is fair to regard your take on a piece of literature as valid, however, that doesn't mean you need only consider your own opinions. Listening to what your instructor and classmates have to say is equally important, especially when they disagree with you. If your positions have value, so do theirs. Perhaps they have seen something you missed, or perhaps they consider crucial something that you had dismissed as unimportant. You may find your first impressions shifting during these discussions, or you may find them solidifying. Either of these outcomes is a good sign that you're learning. The most important thing you bring to a literary discussion is a willingness to share your own perspectives while remaining open to the possibility of learning from others.

Attentive listeners tend to make the best note-takers, and having good class notes will prove incredibly helpful when you sit down to write your papers. This important skill will be covered in the next chapter.

LITERATURE AND ENJOYMENT

You may have noticed that little has been said so far about the idea that reading and writing about literature can also be fun. Some students really enjoy reading imaginative literature and writing papers about it. If you're in that group, you're lucky; your literature class will be fun and interesting for you, and—not incidentally—you'll probably do good work in the course. If you've never been fond of reading and writing about literature, though, you might spend a little time thinking about why some of your classmates enjoy this sort of work as well as what you might do to increase your own enjoyment of literature and investment in the writing process. You'll be happier and write better papers if you can put aside any previous negative experiences with literature and writing you may have had and approach your task with a positive mindset. As you are introduced to new authors, new characters and settings, and new ideas, your literature class may surprise you. It could even end up being a favorite.

CHAPTER 2

The Role of Good Reading

Writing about literature begins, of course, with reading, so it stands to reason that good reading is the first step toward successful writing. But what exactly is "good reading"? Good reading, generally speaking, is not fast reading. In fact, often the best advice a student can receive about reading is to *slow down*. Reading well is all about paying attention, and you can't pay attention if you're texting a friend as you read or racing to get through an assignment and move on to "more important" things. If you make a point of giving yourself plenty of time and minimizing your distractions, you'll get more out of your reading and probably enjoy it more as well.

THE VALUE OF REREADING

The best reading is often rereading, and the best readers are those who are willing to go back and reread a piece of literature again and again. It is not uncommon for professional literary critics—who are, after all, some of the most skilled readers—to read a particular poem, story, or play literally dozens of times before they feel equipped to write about it. And well-written literature rewards this willingness to reread, allowing readers to continue seeing new things with each reading. If you have a favorite book you return to over and over, or a favorite song you like to listen to again and again, you intuitively understand this truth. Realistically, of course, you will not have the time to read every assigned piece many times before discussing it in class or preparing to write about it, but you should not give up or feel frustrated if you fail to "get" a piece of literature on the first reading. Be prepared to go back and reread key sections, or even a whole work, if doing so could help with your understanding.

CRITICAL READING

The sort of reading that works best with imaginative literature—or any other complex writing—is sometimes called *active reading* or *critical reading*, though *critical* here implies not fault-finding but rather thoughtful consideration. Much of the reading we do in everyday life is passive and noncritical. We glance at street signs to see where we are; we check a sports website to find out how our favorite team is doing; we read packages for information about the products we use. And in general, we take in all this information passively, without questioning it or looking for deeper meaning. For many kinds of reading, this is perfectly appropriate. It would hardly make sense to ask, "*Why* is this Pine Street?" or "What do they *mean* when they say there are twelve ounces of soda in this can?" There is, however, another type of reading, one that involves asking critical questions and probing more deeply into the meaning of what we read. This is the kind of reading most appropriate to imaginative literature (especially if we intend to discuss or write about that literature later).

THE MYTH OF "HIDDEN MEANING"

There is a persistent myth in literature classes that the purpose of reading is to scour a text for "hidden meaning." Do not be taken in by this myth. In fact, many instructors dislike the phrase *hidden meaning*, which has unpleasant and inaccurate connotations. First, it suggests a sort of willful subterfuge on the part of the author, a deliberate attempt to make his or her work difficult to understand or to exclude the reader. Second, it makes the process of reading sound like digging for buried treasure rather than a systematic intellectual process. Finally, the phrase implies that a text has a single, true meaning and that communication and understanding move in one direction only: from the crafty author to the searching reader.

In truth, the meanings in literary texts are not hidden, and your job as a reader is not to root around for them. Rather, if a text is not immediately accessible to you, it is because you need to read more actively, and meaning will then emerge in a collaborative effort as you work *with* the text to create a consistent interpretation. (This is the basis of *reader-response criticism*, which is explained on pages 181–182.) Obviously, active reading requires effort. If you find this sort of reading hard, take that as a good sign. It means you're paying the sort of attention that a well-crafted poem, story, or play requires of a reader. You also should not assume that English teachers have a key that allows them to unlock the one secret truth of a text. If, as is often the case, your instructor sees more or different meanings in a piece of literature than you do, this is because he or she is trained to read actively and has probably spent much more time than you have with literature in general and more time with the particular text assigned to you.

Questions for Active Reading:
FICTION

- *The plot, simply put, is the series of events that transpire in a story. How would you summarize the plot of each story? What, if anything, makes it difficult to do so?*

- *Who, in your opinion, are the most sympathetic characters? Who are the most antagonistic? What kinds of information do we learn about the emotional lives of these characters? How do they grow, develop, or change their minds?*

- *What is the point of view of the story? If the author has chosen a first-person or omniscient narration, what are the advantages and disadvantages of those choices?*

- *How would you describe the setting of each story? What details of setting contribute to the tone or atmosphere of the story?*

- *How would you describe the style of writing in each story? Is the prose formal? Casual? Archaic? Conversational? Melodramatic? Be as specific as possible, and note examples that bolster your claims.*

- *What kinds of symbols recur in each story? Are they fanciful? Are they ordinary? Are they conventional? Or are they surprising? How do they move the narrative forward?*

- *All good short stories use vivid physical details and images to bring the story to life. Which details are most memorable to you? How do they affect your interpretation of the characters and events?*

- *What insights do you gather from this story? Do you learn something? Does the author challenge your value system? Do the characters undergo a transformation that is surprising, troubling, or inspiring, and what does that reveal about the story itself?*

ACTIVE READING

Annotating

If the first suggestions for active reading are to slow down and to know that a second (or even a third) reading is in order, the next suggestion is to read with a pen or pencil in hand in order to annotate your text and take notes. If you look inside a literature textbook belonging to your instructor or to an advanced literature student, chances are you'll see something of a mess—words and passages circled or underlined, comments and questions scrawled in the margins (technically called *marginalia*), and unexplained punctuation marks or other symbols decorating the pages. You should not interpret this as disrespect for the text or author or as a sign of a disordered mind. It is simply textual annotation, and it means that someone has been engaged in active reading. Perhaps an extreme example is the poet and critic Samuel Taylor Coleridge, who was famous for annotating not only his own books but also those he borrowed from friends—a habit unlikely to secure a friendship—and his marginalia actually make up one entire volume of his collected works.

If you are not accustomed to textual annotation, it may be hard to know where to begin. There is no single, widely used system of annotation, and you will almost certainly begin to develop your own techniques as you practice active reading. Here, however, are a few tips to get you started:

- **Underline, circle, or highlight passages that strike you as particularly important.** These may be anything from single words to whole paragraphs—but stick to those points in the text that really stand out, the briefer and more specific, the better. Don't worry that you need to find *the* most crucial parts of a poem, play, or story. Everyone sees things a little differently, so just note what makes an impression on *you*.

- **Make notes in the margins as to *why* certain points strike you.** Don't just underline; jot down at least a word or two in the margin to remind yourself what you were thinking when you chose to highlight a particular point. It may seem obvious to you at the moment, but when you return to the text in two weeks to write your paper, you may not remember.

- **Ask questions of the text.** Perhaps the most important aspect of active reading is the practice of asking critical questions of a text. Nobody — not even the most experienced literary critic — understands everything about a literary text immediately, and noting where you are confused or doubtful is an important first step toward resolving any confusion. Types of questions are offered below for each genre, but upon first reading just remember that any point of confusion is fair game, from character **motivation** (*"Why would she do that?"*), to cultural or historical references (*"Where is Xanadu?"*) or to the definitions of individual words (*"Meaning?"*). Most likely, you will eventually want to propose some possible answers, but on a first reading of the text it's enough to note that you have questions.

- **Talk back to the text.** Occasionally, something in a literary text may strike you as suspicious, offensive, or just plain wrong. Just because a story, poem, or play appears in a textbook does not mean that its author is above criticism. Try to keep an open mind and realize that there may be an explanation that would satisfy your criticism, but if you think an author has made a misstep, don't be afraid to make note of your opinion.

- **Look for unusual features of language.** In creating a mood and making a point, literary works rely much more heavily than do purely informational texts on features of language such as **style** and imagery. As a reader of literature, then, you need to heighten your awareness of style. Look for patterns of images, repeated words or phrases, and any other unusual stylistic features — right down to idiosyncratic grammar or punctuation — and make note of them in your marginalia.

- **Develop your own system of shorthand.** Annotating a text, while it obviously takes time, shouldn't become a burden or slow your reading too much, so keep your notes and questions short and to the point. Sometimes all you need is an exclamation point to indicate an important passage. An underlined term combined with a question mark in the margin can remind you that you didn't immediately understand what a word meant. Be creative, but try also to be consistent so you'll know later what you meant by a particular symbol or comment.

Student Rachel McCarthy was assigned to read William Butler Yeats's poem "The Second Coming." Here are some of the annotations she made as she read the poem:

WILLIAM BUTLER YEATS [1865–1939]

The Second Coming

Turning and turning in the widening gyre
The falcon cannot hear the falconer;
Things fall apart; the centre cannot hold;
Mere anarchy is loosed upon the world,
The blood-dimmed tide is loosed, and everywhere
The ceremony of innocence is drowned;
The best lack all conviction, while the worst
Are full of passionate intensity.

Surely some revelation is at hand;
Surely the Second Coming is at hand.
The Second Coming! Hardly are those words out
When a vast image out of *Spiritus Mundi*
Troubles my sight: somewhere in sands of the desert
A shape with lion body and the head of a man,
A gaze blank and pitiless as the sun,
Is moving its slow thighs, while all about it
Reel shadows of the indignant desert birds.
The darkness drops again; but now I know
That twenty centuries of stony sleep
Were vexed to nightmare by a rocking cradle,
And what rough beast, its hour come round at last,
Slouches towards Bethlehem to be born?

Gyre: a circular or spiral motion or form, especially a giant circular oceanic surface current (Merriam-Webster).

Possible reference to the biblical plagues of Egypt.

What is this ceremony? Baptism?

Heavy repetition in this passage.

Latin word for "world spirit" — a phrase used to describe the collective soul and memories of the universe.

Like a sphinx?

The sun can be equated with the eye of the heavens — has God turned his back on humanity?

Possible allusion to darkness dropping over Jerusalem when Jesus died.

Presumably the antichrist.

[1921]

Rachel's annotations cover everything from major points of content, like Yeats's allusion to the sphinx and the definition of *gyre*, to her observations on Yeats's use of repetition in the second stanza. Having annotated the poem in this way, Rachel was ready to participate in discussions both in the classroom and online, and later she had some good starting notes when she decided to write a paper about the poem.

Questions for Active Reading:
POETRY

- *Wallace Stevens once said that "the poem is the cry of its occasion." What occasion forced this poem into utterance? Why did the poet have to write it? What other occasions do you see throughout this poem?*

- *Who is the main speaker of the poem? How would this poem sound if it were spoken from another perspective? For example, how would Robert Browning's dramatic monologue "My Last Duchess" (p. 69) sound if it were spoken by the Duke's guest?*

- *For whom is the speaker writing the poem? What evidence do you see for this reading?*

- *Imagery creates a sensory experience on the page. How does the poetry use imagery to make you feel the experience in the poem?*

- *How is the poem arranged on the page? How would you describe the shape of the stanzas? The shape of the lines? How long or short are the lines? Why does this matter to the content of the poem?*

- *Where do you see patterns of repetition? In shape, in language, in image? What effect does this achieve?*

- *What has the speaker realized (or not realized) by the end of the poem? Where does the poem take you, and how do you get there? Most poems include a turn, or an* aha *moment, when the poet makes a shift toward discovery.*

- *How would you describe the language of the poem? What kind of diction does the speaker use? What verb tense? What references?*

Note-Taking

Note-taking is a good idea, especially if you are reading a difficult text or one about which you expect to be writing, to keep a notebook handy as you read, a place to make notes that would be too long or complex to fit in the margins. What should these notes contain? Essentially, they should be more extensive versions of your marginalia. You should note any unusual repetitions or juxtapositions, as well as anything that surprises you or frustrates your expectations as you read. Note passages that seem particularly crucial, or particularly confusing (using page numbers, and perhaps placing an asterisk or other symbol in the margins), and write a few sentences explaining why these stood out for you. Ask plenty of questions, as explained later in this chapter.

You might want to use the same notebook that you keep with you in class so that you can make reference to your class notes while reading at home and bring the insights from your reading to your class discussions. In class, write down any information your instructor writes on the board or projects using PowerPoint or other presentation software. If he or she thought it was important enough to write down, you probably should, too. Your class notes should include new terminology or vocabulary, as well as any point the instructor repeats more than once or twice. Be sure to also take note of comments by your classmates that seem especially salient to your evolving understanding of the literature, particularly points you disagree with or would not have thought of on your own. Just be sure to distinguish which ideas in your notes are yours and which you read or heard from someone else. It may be obvious to you now, but can you guarantee that a month from now, when you're writing a paper, you'll remember who produced that gem of insight?

Remember that the best note-takers are not necessarily those who have amassed the most pages of notes at the end of the term. Good notes don't need to be well-reasoned paragraphs or even complete sentences. In fact, they seldom are. The key to taking good notes is to take them quickly, with minimal interruption to your reading or participation in a discussion. As with annotating texts, try to develop your own shorthand for note-taking. Just be sure that you write enough to jog your memory when you return to the notes days, weeks, or even months later. Try to be consistent in what and how you abbreviate. One specific piece of advice, though: it's a good idea to jot down page numbers in your notes, referring to the specific lines or passages under discussion. That way, you'll have no problem matching up the notes with the texts to which they refer.

Questions for Active Reading:
DRAMA

- *What actually happens within the frame of the play? What transpired before the play started? What do you speculate will happen once the play is over?*

- *Every character has unique attributes and relationships with other characters. What do you learn about each character through their interaction with others? How do the characters speak? Do they use slang? A regional dialect? Does someone hesitate or speak in fits and starts? What do characters withhold or reveal through their dialogue?*

- *Setting can determine how characters act and what obstacles may stand in their way. What does the setting of the play reveal to you? For example, how does the setting in Susan Glaspell's* Trifles *(p. 123)—an abandoned farmhouse in a farming community—affect the series of events in the play?*

- *Scenes are the building blocks of any dramatic text. Can you identify each scene? What does each one accomplish?*

- *Typically, dramatic texts establish tension right away. What is the central tension of the dramatic text? Where do you first learn of the tension or problem? Does it get resolved by the end of the play? If not, why not?*

- *You can tell a lot about a play based on how the writer manipulates time. How does time move in the play? Does it move sequentially? Are there flashbacks? Speculations about the future? How long does it take for time to transpire in the play? How do you know?*

- *Are there moments of dramatic irony—that is, moments in which you as an audience member know something that the characters onstage do not? Why does the playwright create this gap in a character's knowledge? How does it affect you as a viewer?*

- *What does this play reveal about the culture in which it was produced?*

- *What insights do you gather from this dramatic text? Does the play challenge your value system? Do the characters undergo a transformation that is surprising, troubling, or inspiring, and what does that reveal about the play itself?*

Journal Keeping

You may be assigned to keep a reading journal for your class. Of course, you should follow your instructor's guidelines, but if you aren't sure what to write in a reading journal, think of it as a place to go a step further than you do in your annotations and notes. Try out possible answers, preferably several different ones, to the questions you have raised. Expand your ideas from single phrases and sentences into entire paragraphs, and see how they hold up under this deeper probing. Although a reading journal is substantially different from a personal journal or diary, it can at times contain reflections on any connections you make between a piece of literature and your own life and ideas. Some instructors ask students to respond to their readings with internet resources, including course management systems, e-mail messages, or blog entries. These platforms allow you to build an archive of your responses so that you can easily return to them when you begin writing a draft of your paper; in addition, you can respond to other students as they develop their ideas. Here is Rachel's response to "The Second Coming" that she posted on the course management system for her class:

Forum: The Second Coming
Date: 10 Feb 2020 22:15
Author: McCarthy, Rachel
Subject: Imagery and Allusion

Yeats's apocalyptic vision of the future is a fascinating departure from that described in the Book of Revelation. Here, supernatural forces from heaven and hell do not precipitate the End Times with fire raining down from the sky; rather, the first stanza illustrates the slow yet inevitable unraveling of the world as things spiral out of control. The orderly nature of the world that we take for granted on a day-to-day basis is only tenuously restraining chaos and disaster.

In a similar vein, I think some of the anxiety I felt while reading this poem can be attributed to the fact that the "rough beast" (21) is just here, on Earth, biding its time in some remote corner of a desert. And, not only does it begin on Earth, but it might possibly begin with us. Yeats predicts a generation of people where "the best lack all conviction, while the worst / Are full of passionate intensity" (7–8). This can mean one of two things: either people have given up on righteousness and support evil willingly (or are too spineless to resist), or there's no distinction between people who are passionate about doing good and those who passionately commit evil. I honestly don't know which is the more chilling interpretation.

Finally, for all of Yeats's vivid imagery about the blood-dimmed tide and the beast in the desert, he also employs ambiguity to great effect. Going back to Revelation, the beast is described at great length as an amalgam of animal parts with seven heads and ten horns; by contrast, Yeats's "rough beast" leaves us to fill in the blanks with whatever terrifying image our imaginations can come up with. That dreaded feeling of the unknown, as this great, hulking shadow of a monster draws ominously towards a sleepy little village, is what makes Yeats's "Second Coming" such a well-crafted exercise in horror by subverting our expectations.

In this brief response, Rachel focuses on the differences between the apocalypse that she sees in the Book of Revelation with the one that Yeats describes in his poem. She focuses on Yeats's imagery and allusions in order to better understand why this poem is so chilling.

This kind of response will serve Rachel well when it's time to generate a thesis for her paper on the subject. Even if your instructor doesn't require online forum participation or a journal for your class, many students find keeping a journal a useful tool for getting more out of their reading, not to mention a wealth of material to draw from when they sit down to write a paper.

Using Reference Materials

Many students are reluctant to use the dictionary or encyclopedia while reading, thinking they should be able to figure out the meanings of words from their context and not wanting to interrupt their reading. But the simple truth is that not all words are definable from context alone, and you'll get much more out of your reading if you are willing to make the small effort involved in looking up unfamiliar words. If you are reading John Donne's "A Valediction: Forbidding Mourning" and you don't know what the word *valediction* means, you're starting at a big disadvantage. A quick look in a print or online dictionary would tell you that a valediction is a speech given at a time of parting (like the one a *valedictorian* gives at a graduation ceremony). Armed with that simple piece of information, you begin reading Donne's poem already knowing that it is about leaving someone or something, and understanding the poem becomes much simpler. Notice that the annotations for the Yeats poem earlier in the chapter include a definition of *gyre*.

An encyclopedia like *Britannica Online* (an online subscription service available at most university libraries) can also be a useful tool. As you're reading Yeats's poem, if you want to read his biography, *Britannica Online* can provide biographical and cultural context for his life and work. Or, if you want to learn more about the meter of the poem, you could look up "iambic pentameter" to develop an understanding of its use, or "blank verse" to learn about the cultural context of the verse form. *Britannica Online* often provides a bibliography for further reading, so it can be a good place to start your research.

ASKING CRITICAL QUESTIONS OF LITERATURE

Questions about literature fall into one of four categories — questions about the text, about the author, about the cultural context of the work, and about the reader. We'll discuss each of these in the next few pages.

Questions about the Text

Questions about a text focus on issues such as **genre**, **structure**, language, and style. Queries regarding the text can sometimes, though not always, be answered with a deeper examination of the story, poem, or play at hand. You might ask about the presence of certain images — or about their absence, if you have reason to expect them and find that they are not there. Sometimes authors juxtapose images or language in startling or unexpected ways, and you might ask about the purpose and effect of such **juxtaposition**. You might wonder about the meanings of specific words in the context of the work. (This is especially true with older works of literature, as meanings evolve and change over time, and a word you know today might have had a very different definition in the past.) When looking at a poem, you might inquire about the purpose and effect of sound, rhythm, rhyme, and so forth.

Your previous experiences are a big help here, including both your experiences of reading literature and your experiences in everyday life. You know from personal experience how you expect people to think and act in certain situations, and you can compare these expectations to the literature. What might motivate the characters or persons to think and act as they do? Your previous reading has likewise set up expectations for you. How does the text fulfill or frustrate these expectations? What other literary pieces does this remind you of? What images seem arresting or unexpected? Where do the words seem particularly powerful, strange, or otherwise noteworthy?

Notice some of the questions one reader asked in his annotations upon first reading Ben Jonson's "On My First Son."

BEN JONSON   [1572–1637]

On My First Son

Why is hope for his child a "sin"?

Farewell, thou child of my right hand, and joy;
My sin was too much hope of thee, loved boy:

The rhyme in ll. 1–2 aligns "joy" with "boy."

Seven years thou' wert lent to me, and I thee pay,
Exacted by thy fate, on the just day.

Why does the speaker treat the son like a bank transaction?

O could I lose all father now! for why

The word just has two meanings: exact and fair. Which does the poet mean?

Will man lament the state he should envy,
To have so soon 'scaped world's and flesh's rage,
And, if no other misery, yet age?
Rest in soft peace, and asked, say, "Here doth lie
Ben Jonson his best piece of poetry."

What does he mean by this line? (confusing)

For whose sake henceforth all his vows be such
As what he loves may never like too much.

Here the poem works as a kind of epitaph on a tombstone. Is it actually the boy's epitaph?

The questions the student asks of the poem are, for the most part, substantial and difficult, and they will require a good deal of thinking and interpretation to get to an answer. These are the sorts of questions that prompt good discussions and good writing.

Questions about the Author

When thinking about the connection between authors and the works they produce, two contradictory impulses come into play. One is the desire to ignore the biography of the author entirely and focus solely on the work at hand, and the other is to look closely at an author's life to see what might have led him or her to write a particular poem, story, or play. It is easy to understand the first impulse. After all, we are not likely to ask an author what a certain line in a play means or whether an image in a story is supposed to be read symbolically. The work of literature is what we have before us, and it should stand or fall on its own merits. This was, in fact, one of the principal tenets of **New Criticism**, a method of interpretation that dominated literary criticism for much of the twentieth century and is discussed on page 174.

We cannot deny, however, that a writer's life does affect that writer's expression. Age, gender, religious beliefs, family structure, and many other factors have an impact on everything in an author's life from topic choice to word choice. Therefore, it is sometimes appropriate to ask questions about an author as we try to come to a better understanding of a piece of literature. It is crucial, however, that we remember that not everything an author writes is to be taken at surface value. For instance, if the narrator or principal character of a story is beaten or neglected by his parents, we should not jump to the conclusion that the author was an abused child. And if this character then goes on to justify his own actions by pointing to the abuse, we should also not assume that the author endorses this justification. In other words, we must distinguish between narrative voice and the actual author as well as between what is written and what is meant.

This separation of biography and narrative is relatively easy with stories and plays that we know to be fiction; just because a character says something doesn't necessarily mean the author believes it. Poetry is a little trickier, though, because it has the reputation of being straight from the heart. Not every poem, however, is an accurate representation of the respective author's thoughts or beliefs. To give just two examples, T. S. Eliot's "The Love Song of J. Alfred Prufrock" (p. 112) voices the thoughts of the fictional Prufrock, not of Eliot himself, and many of the poems of Robert Browning are **dramatic monologues**, delivered by speakers very different from Browning himself, including murderous noblemen and corrupt clergy. (An example of such a monologue is "My Last Duchess" on pages 69–71.)

Questions about the Cultural Context

We are all creatures of a particular time and place, and nobody, no matter how unique and iconoclastic, is immune to the subtle and pervasive force of social history. Many appropriate questions about literature, in this case, involve the **cultural context** of the work. What was going on in history at the time a piece of literature was written? Were there wars or other forms of social disruption? What was the standard of living for most people in the author's society? What was day-to-day life like? What were the typical religious beliefs and traditions? How was society organized in terms of power relations, work expectations, and educational possibilities? How about typical family structure? Did extended families live together? What were the expected gender roles inside (and outside) the family? All of these issues, and many more besides, have an impact on how authors see the world and how they respond to it in their writing.

As you read and ask questions of literature, you have another cultural context to be concerned with — your own. How does being a resident of twenty-first-century America affect your reading and understanding? We are every bit as influenced by issues of history, culture, and lifestyle as were authors and readers of the past, but it is harder for us to see this, since the dominant way of living tends to seem "natural" or even "universal." Indeed, one of the great benefits of reading literature is that it teaches us about history and helps us understand and appreciate diverse cultures, not the least of which is our own.

In asking and answering the following questions about Ben Jonson's culture (seventeenth-century England), an attentive reader of "On My First Son" will also note features of our own present-day society, in which childhood death is relatively rare, family roles may be different, and religious attitudes and beliefs are considerably more diverse.

- How common was childhood death in the seventeenth century? What was the average life expectancy?
- Typically, how involved were fathers in young children's lives at the time?
- Is the quotation in the poem (lines 9–10) the boy's epitaph?
- What exactly does Jonson mean by the "world's and flesh's rage"?
- How common was poetry on this topic? How "original" was Jonson's poem? How does his poem tap into a larger elegiac tradition, in Jonson's time and beyond?
- What attitudes about God and heaven were common back then? What was the conception of sin?

Questions about the Reader

Except in the case of private diaries, all writing is intended to be read by somebody, and an intended audience can have a big influence on the composition of the writing in question. Think about the differences in tone and structure between a text message you send to a friend and a paper you write for a course, and you'll get some idea of the impact of intended audience on a piece of writing. It is therefore worth considering a work's originally intended readers as you seek to understand a piece more fully. Who were the intended readers? Were they actually the people who read the literature when it was first published? How are readers' expectations fulfilled or disappointed by the structure and content of the literature? How did the original readers react? Was the work widely popular, or did only certain readers enjoy it? Did it have detractors as well? Was there any controversy over the work?

Of course, in addition to the original readers of any work of literature, there are also contemporary readers, including yourself. It is often said that great literature stands the test of time and can cross cultures to speak to many different sorts of people, but your reaction to a work may be very different from that of its original audience, especially if you are far removed from the work by time or culture. In earlier centuries in Europe and America, nearly all educated people were very familiar with the Bible and with stories and myths from Greek and Roman antiquity. Writers, therefore, could assume such knowledge on the part of their readers and make liberal references in their work to stories and characters from these sources. Today, many readers are less familiar with these sources, and we often need the help of footnotes or other study aids to understand such references. So what might have been enjoyable and enlightening for the original readers of a work might sometimes be tedious or frustrating for later readers. If we are to read a work critically, we must keep both past and present audiences in mind.

The first three of the following questions deal with the original audience of "On My First Son," while the final two compare this audience and a contemporary one.

- If childhood death was common in the seventeenth century, how would Jonson's readers have related to the subject of his poem?
- Did Jonson write this for wide circulation, or was it meant just for family and friends?
- Where was the poem first published, and who was likely to read it?
- Do readers with children of their own read the poem differently? Would I?
- Now that childhood death is less common in the United States, do we read this poem differently than past readers might have?

Looking over these questions about Jonson's poem—about the text, the author, the cultural context, and the reader—you will note that there are many differences among them. Some can be answered with a simple yes or no (*Is the quotation the boy's epitaph?*), while others require much more complex responses (*What was the conception of sin in Jonson's time?*). Others are matters of conjecture, opinion, or interpretation (*Do contemporary readers read this poem differently than past readers might have?*). Some can be answered simply by rereading and considering (*How can a child's death ever be considered fair?*), while others require discussion (*Do readers with children respond to the poem differently?*) or research (*Where was the poem first published?*).

For some inquiries, you may have tentative answers, as did the reader who asked these questions when she proposed both God and fate as potential candidates for who "lent" the child to the father. However, you won't be able to answer others at first. If you are genuinely curious about any of them, do a little informal research to begin formulating answers. Some basic information can be found in the brief biographies or notes about authors that appear in most textbooks. There you could learn, for instance, the dates of Jonson's birth and death and some basic facts about his life and family. A quick look at a reputable reference work or website could provide still more valuable background information, like the fact that Jonson also lost his first daughter and that he wrote a poem about her death as well.

CHECKLIST FOR GOOD READING

Questions to ask as you read and think about literary texts:

- ☐ Have you slowed down and reread complex passages several times?
- ☐ Are you looking up difficult words in the dictionary to see if they have secondary meanings?
- ☐ Are you annotating the text by underlining key phrases? Writing questions or concerns in the margins?
- ☐ Are you taking your reading to the next level by asking how or why these passages are compelling to you?
- ☐ Are you marking those places in the text that make you feel uncomfortable, or present a worldview that feels strange to you?
- ☐ After you read, are you taking notes so that you can keep track of your ideas?
- ☐ Have you identified the **genre** of the text? Have you described its style and **tone**?
- ☐ Have you checked *Britannica Online* or other reference sources to learn more about the author and his or her cultural context?
- ☐ Have you reflected on your perspective as a twenty-first-century reader, and how that might affect your interpretation of literature from another time period?

Having simply formulated some questions, you've already gone a long way toward understanding and interpreting a poem or other work of literature. If you bring such a list of questions with you to class, you will be more than ready to contribute to the discussion, and when the time comes to write an essay, you will have a rich mine of source material from which to draw.

CHAPTER 3

The Writing Process

Experts often divide the writing process into three major components: prewriting, drafting, and revision (which includes editing). Bear in mind, though, that the process for most people is not as linear as this suggests, and the three components don't always happen in a straightforward fashion. For instance, you might begin revising a partial draft before completing the drafting process. Or you may find yourself stuck at a fairly late point in the draft and decide to revisit your prewriting. Don't think that these three steps need to be completed one at a time. Different projects will likely call for different strategies, and you'll enjoy the process more if you allow yourself to go back and forth between the steps according to the needs of the particular assignment you're trying to complete.

PREWRITING

Prewriting is everything that you do before beginning an actual draft of your paper. It includes annotating and questioning texts, taking notes and participating in class, and discussing the assignment with your instructor and/or classmates. It also includes specific topics covered in this chapter: choosing a topic, developing an argument and a thesis, gathering support, and proposing a paper's organizational strategy.

Choosing a Topic

Obviously, your choice of a topic for your paper is of key importance, since everything else follows from that first decision. Your instructor may assign a specific topic, or the choice may be left to you. The most important piece of advice for choosing a topic is to write about something that genuinely interests you. If your instructor gives your class a choice, chances are that he or she really wants to see a variety of topics and approaches and expects you to find a topic that works for *you*.

Even if your instructor assigns a fairly specific topic, you still need to spend a little time thinking about and working with it. You want your paper to stand out from the rest, and you should do whatever you can to make the assignment your own. When you receive an assignment, give some thought as to how it might relate to your own interests and how you might call upon your background and knowledge to approach the topic in fresh and interesting ways.

Finally, if you've put in some thought and effort but still don't know what to write about, remember that you do not need to go it alone—seek out guidance and help. Talk with other students in your class and see what they have decided to write about; although of course you don't want simply to copy someone else's topic, hearing what others think can often spark a fresh idea. And don't forget your instructor. Most teachers are more than happy to spend a little time helping you come up with a topic and an approach that will help you write a good paper.

Developing an Argument

With the possible exception of a *summary* (a brief recap of a text's most important points), all writing about literature is, to some degree, a form of argument. Before proceeding, though, let's dispel some of the negative connotations of the word *argument*. In everyday usage, this term can connote a heated verbal fight, and it suggests two (or more) people growing angry and, often, becoming less articulate and more abusive as time passes. It suggests combat and implies that the other party in the process is an opponent. In this sort of argument, there are winners and losers.

Clearly this is not what we have in mind when we say you will be writing argumentatively about literature. Used in a different, more traditional sense, *argument* refers to a writer's, or speaker's, attempt to establish the validity of a given position. In other words, when you write a paper, you work to convince your reader that what you are saying is valid and persuasive. The reader is not the enemy, not someone whose ideas are to be crushed and refuted, but rather a person whose thoughts and feelings you have a chance to affect. You are not arguing *against* your reader; rather, you are using your argumentative abilities to *help* your reader see the logic and value of your position.

THE THESIS

To begin writing a literary argument, then, you must take a position and have a point to make. This principal point will be the *thesis* of your paper. It is important to distinguish between a topic and a thesis; your topic is the issue or area upon which you will focus your attention, and your thesis is a statement *about* this topic.

Here is an example of a topic for William Butler Yeats's "The Second Coming" from a student journal:

Topic: I am interested in how Yeats uses imagery of the Apocalypse.

Here is an example of a thesis statement for a paper on this topic:

Thesis: "The Second Coming" disrupts Christian models of the Apocalypse, and in doing so challenges the reader to grapple with the uncomfortable prospect that the world as we understand it right now will soon face utter annihilation.

It might help to phrase your thesis as a complete sentence in which the topic is the subject, followed by a predicate that makes a firm statement or claim regarding your topic. This is your **thesis statement**, and it will probably appear toward the beginning of your paper. The foremost purpose of a paper, then, is to explain, defend, and ultimately prove the truth of its thesis.

Keep the following guidelines in mind as you think about a tentative thesis for your paper:

- **Your thesis should be both clear and specific.** The purpose of a thesis is to serve as a guide to both the reader and the writer, so it needs to be understandable and to point clearly to the specific aspects of the literature that you will discuss.

- **Your thesis should be relevant.** The claim you make should not only interest you as a writer but also give your reader a reason to keep reading by sparking his or her interest and desire to know more. Not every paper is going to change lives or minds, of course, but you should at least state your thesis in such a way that your reader won't have the most dreaded of responses: "Who cares?"

- **Your thesis should be debatable.** Since the purpose of an argumentative paper is to convince a reader that your thesis is correct (or at least that it has merit), it cannot simply be an irrefutable fact. A good thesis will be something that a reasonable person, having read the literature, might disagree with or might not have considered at all. It should give you something to prove.

- **Your thesis should be original.** Again, originality does not imply that every thesis you write must be a brilliant gem that nobody but you could have discovered. But it should be something you have thought about independently, and it should avoid clichés, contain something of you, and do more than parrot back something said in your class or written in your textbook.

- **You should be able to state your thesis as a complete sentence.** This sentence, generally referred to as the *thesis statement*, should first identify your topic and then make a claim about it. (Occasionally, especially for longer papers with more complex ideas behind them, you will need more than one sentence to state your thesis clearly. Even in these cases, though, the complete thesis must both identify the topic and make a claim about it.)

- **Your thesis should be stated in strong, unambiguous language.** Avoid lead-up phrases like "In this paper, I will prove . . .," "In my opinion . . .," or "I think . . .," If you have a point to prove, just prove it. Keep the reader focused on the topic. Language like this weakens your sentence.

- **Your thesis should be appropriate to the assignment.** This may seem obvious, but as we work with literature, taking notes, asking questions, and beginning to think about topics and theses, it is possible to lose sight of the assignment as it was presented. After you have come up with a tentative thesis, it's a good idea to go back and review the assignment as your instructor gave it, making sure your paper will fulfill its requirements.

Let us take a look at how two students arrived at strong, workable theses for their papers. Rachel McCarthy knew that she wanted to write about how William Butler Yeats dealt with imagery in his poetry. Her first attempt at a thesis, however, was far too weak and general:

> Yeats's poems feature some of the most haunting imagery ever written.

This is not so much a thesis statement as an observation and opinion. All we know from reading it is that Rachel is interested in Yeats's powerful imagery. She needs a thesis that is both more specific and more controversial:

> Yeats's poems use imagery of the apocalypse in unconventional ways.

This version is a little better because it is more focused, but Rachel hasn't said anything contestable yet. Here is the final version of Rachel's thesis:

> Paul Deane suggests that Yeats's "widening gyre" is a metaphor for historical change that reveals an underlying unity in the poem; however, I would argue that in "The Second Coming," Yeats uses imagery of disunity and chaos in order to create a feeling of horror of "The Second Coming," thus exploiting readers' fears of the unknown.

Here we have a much stronger thesis. It limits the paper's scope by focusing on a single poem, it makes an assertion that differs from a scholarly source, and it shows why this point is significant to a reader (because we might want to understand how Yeats envisioned the Apocalypse).

Here is one more example of the process of refining and developing a thesis. When she first decided to write about the male characters in two nineteenth-century stories, Melanie Smith came up with the following thesis:

> The husbands in the stories "The Yellow Wallpaper" by Charlotte Perkins Gilman and "The Story of an Hour" by Kate Chopin are very controlling of their wives.

This is not an adequate thesis because it is simply a statement of fact, something that will be immediately obvious to anyone who has read the stories. It left Melanie with nothing to defend, no point to prove, so she gave it a little more thought and refined her tentative thesis:

> Though the husbands in "The Yellow Wallpaper" and "The Story of an Hour" are controlling, they are not really as bad as they first appear.

At this point, the writer is definitely moving in the right direction. This version shows that she has a particular interpretation and a point to make, one that is not necessarily shared by everyone who reads the stories. However, it still doesn't give a reader much guidance about what to expect in the paper. In the end, Melanie needed two sentences to get her thesis right:

> By modern standards, the husbands of the two protagonists, particularly John in "The Yellow Wallpaper," seem almost unbearably controlling of their wives. From the vantage point of the late nineteenth century, however, their behavior looks quite different.

This version is much clearer and more precise. After reading this thesis, we are much more focused and have a good sense of what to expect in the paper as a whole. (See pages 102–105 for Melanie's full essay.)

You will note that in this discussion the phrase *tentative thesis* has come up several times. The word *tentative* is important. As you start to gather support and to write your paper, your thesis will help you focus clearly on your task and sort out which of your ideas, observations, and questions are relevant to the project at hand. But you should keep an open mind as well, realizing that your thesis is likely to evolve as you write. You are likely to change the focus in subtle or not so subtle ways, and you might even change your mind completely as you write and therefore need to create a new thesis from scratch. If this happens, don't regard it as a failure. On the contrary, it means you have succeeded in learning something genuine from the experience of writing, and that is what a literature course is all about.

Gathering Support for Your Thesis

Once you have crafted a tentative thesis, it is time to think about the evidence or support you will need to convince your reader of the claim's validity. But what exactly counts as support? What can you include in your paper as evidence that your thesis is true? Essentially, all support comes from one of three sources:

- **The text itself.** It is not enough to *say* that a certain piece of literature says or means a certain thing. You will need to *show* this by summarizing, paraphrasing, or quoting the literature itself.
- **Other people's ideas.** Chances are you will find a lot of useful material for your paper if you pay attention to easily available sources of ideas from other readers. These include the notes and biographical information in your textbooks, research conducted online or in the library, lectures and discussions in class, and even informal conversations about the literature with your friends and classmates.
- **Your own thoughts.** Remember that although you may want to integrate ideas and information from a variety of sources, your paper is yours and as such should reflect *your* thinking. The most indispensable source of material for your paper is your own mind; your own thoughts and words should always carry the heaviest weight in any paper you write.

One of the best ways to gather supporting ideas for your paper is *brainstorming*. You can brainstorm—alone or with classmates—even before settling on your topic and thesis, to explore the many possible threads that you could follow in your writing. When brainstorming to gather evidence, the idea is to write down, very quickly, every idea that comes to you, every possible idea that might be included in the draft of your paper. Don't censor yourself during this process. Allow yourself to write down everything that interests, puzzles, or delights you. Later you will have ample opportunity to prune your list of repetitions, tangents, or weaker ideas. For the time being, just let the ideas flow, and get as many as you can down on a piece of paper or as you can down in your notes.

ORGANIZING YOUR PAPER

Once you've determined what evidence to use, it is time to begin sorting and organizing it. The principle for organizing any paper is the sequence of paragraphs, so at this stage you should be thinking at the level of paragraph content. Remember that each paragraph should contain one main idea and sufficient evidence and explanation to support that idea. When added together, these paragraph-level ideas lead a reader to your paper's ultimate point—your thesis. So the first stage of organizing the content of your essay is to cluster together similar ideas in order to begin shaping the substance of individual paragraphs. The second stage is to determine the order in which these paragraphs will appear.

For most writers, creating some version of an outline is the best way to approach the task of organizing evidence into a logical sequence for a paper. In the past, you may have been asked to write a formal outline, complete with roman numerals and capital letters. If this technique has been helpful in organizing your thoughts, by all means continue to use it. For many writers, however, an informal outline works just as well and is less cumbersome. To construct an informal outline, simply jot down a heading that summarizes the topic of each paragraph you intend to write. Then cluster your gathered evidence—quotations or paraphrases from the literature, ideas for analysis, and so on—into groups under the headings.

The following is an example of an informal outline for a paper on Shakespeare's Sonnet 116. (The full paper appears on pages 117–119.) In this outline, the student focuses on the positive and negative language in the poem and how it results in a more interesting definition of love than he had seen in other love poems.

Introduction

    Two kinds of typical love poems: happy and sad

    Sonnet 116 is more complex and interesting

    <u>Tentative thesis</u>: By including both negative and positive images and language, this sonnet gives a complex and realistic definition of love.

Vivid images in poem

    <u>Positive/expected</u>: "star," "ever-fixèd mark," "rosy lips and cheeks"

    <u>Negative/unexpected</u>: "sickle" (deathlike), "wandering bark" (lost boat), "tempests"

Negative language

    <u>Words/phrases</u>: "Let me not," "Love is not," "never," "nor," "no," etc.

    <u>Abstractions</u>: "alteration," "impediments," "error"

Conclusion

    Love never changes

    Shakespeare's definition still works some 400 years later

Obviously, this is not a formal outline. It does, however, group similar items and ideas together, and it gives the writer a basic structure to follow as he moves on to drafting, the next stage of the composing process.

DRAFTING THE PAPER

To recap, you have a topic, a tentative thesis, gathered evidence, and an outline or tentative structure in mind for said evidence. It is time to begin writing your first draft. Every writer has his or her own slightly different process for getting the words down on paper. Some begin at the beginning of the paper and work straight through to the end in a clear, organized fashion. Others begin with the first body paragraph and save the introduction for later. Still others write bits and pieces of the paper out of order and allow the overall structure to emerge at a later time.

Some writers claim that they work better at the last minute and focus better under the pressure of a looming deadline. This, however, is almost always a justification for sloppy work habits, and procrastination rarely if ever results in a superior paper. When habitual procrastinators change their working methods and give themselves more time on a project, they are frequently surprised to discover that the process is more enjoyable and the final product of their efforts better than what they have produced in the past. Start early and work steadily—it will prove more than worth it.

Try writing your first draft fairly quickly. You don't need to get every sentence just right—that's what the revision phase of writing is for. What you want now is just to get as much good raw material as possible into the mix and see what works. Don't worry too much yet about style, transitions, grammar, and so forth. In fact, you don't even need to start at the beginning or work right through to the end. If you get stuck on one part, move on. You can always come back and fill in the gaps later. Introductions can be especially tricky, particularly since you haven't yet finished the essay and don't really know what it is you're introducing. Some writers find it easier to start with the body of the essay, or to write a short, sloppy introduction as a placeholder. You can go back and work on the real introduction when the draft is complete.

Introductions, Conclusions, and Transitions

Ideally, of course, all of the parts of your paper will be equally compelling and polished, but there are certain points in a paper that most often cause trouble for writers and readers, and these points may require a little additional attention on your part. The most typical trouble spots are introductory and concluding paragraphs and the transitional sentences that connect paragraphs. Although there is no one formula to help you navigate these waters, as each writing situation and each paper are different, we offer some general guidelines that can help you think through the problems that might arise in these areas.

Introductions

Essentially, an introduction accomplishes two things: First, it gives a sense of both your topic and your approach to that topic, which is why it is common to make your thesis statement a part of the introduction. Second, an introduction grabs your readers' interest and makes them want to read on and find out what your paper has to say. Some common strategies used in effective introductions are to begin with a probing rhetorical question, a vivid description, or an intriguing quotation. Weak introductions tend to speak in generalities or in philosophical ideas that are only tangentially related to the real topic of your paper. Don't spin your wheels: get specific and get to the point right away.

Consider this introduction from a student essay on Susan Glaspell's *Trifles*:

> What is the relationship between legality and morality? Susan Glaspell's short play *Trifles* asks us to ponder this question, but it provides no clear answers. Part murder mystery, part battle of the sexes, the play makes its readers confront and question many issues about laws, morals, and human relationships. In Mrs. Peters, a sheriff's wife, the play chronicles one woman's moral journey from a certain, unambiguous belief in the law to a more situational view of ethics. Before it is over, this once legally minded woman is even willing to cover up the truth and let someone get away with murder.

The student poses a philosophical question at the very beginning of the paper and then offers a tentative answer. (This paper appears in its entirety on pages 135–138.)

Conclusions

Your conclusion should give your reader something new to think about, a reason not to forget your essay as soon as the reading is done. Some writers like to use the conclusion to return to an idea, a quotation, or an image first raised in the introduction, creating a satisfying feeling of completeness and self-containment.

In the following example from the same student paper, note how the student offers a tentative answer in her conclusion to the question that began the essay:

> In the end, Mrs. Peters gives in to what she believes to be emotionally right rather than what is legally permissible. She collaborates with Mrs. Hale to cover up evidence of the motive and hide the dead canary. Though very little time has gone by, she has undergone a major transformation. She may be, as the county attorney says, "married to the law," but she is also divorced from her old ideals. When she tries to cover up the evidence, a stage direction says she "goes to pieces," and Mrs. Hale has to help her. By the time she pulls herself together, the new woman she is will be a very different person from the old one. She, along with the reader, is now in a world where the relationship between legality and morality is far more complex than she had ever suspected.

Some writers use the conclusion to show the implications of their claims or the connections between the literature and real life. This is your chance to make a good final impression, so don't waste it with simple summary and restatement.

Transitions

Each paragraph is built around a different idea, and the job of the transitions is to show how these separate ideas are related to one another, to make the juxtaposition of two paragraphs seem as logical to a reader as it is to the writer. When you think a transition isn't working effectively, the first question you should ask yourself is, *why* does one paragraph follow another in this particular order? Would it make more sense to change the placement of some paragraphs, or is this really the best organizational strategy for this portion of the paper? Once you know why your paper is structured as it is, transitions become much easier to write, simply making apparent to your audience the connections you already know to be there. As you begin each new paragraph, give some consideration to the links between it and the previous paragraph, and try to make those links explicit in the opening sentence.

REVISING AND EDITING

Once you have a complete, or near-complete, draft, it's time to begin thinking about revision. Try to avoid the common pitfall of thinking of revision as locating and fixing mistakes. Revision is far more than this. Looking at the parts of the word, you can see that *re-vision* means "seeing again," and indeed the revision stage of the writing process is your chance to see your draft anew and make real and substantial improvements to every facet of it, from its organization to its tone to your word choices. Most successful writers will tell you that it is in the revision stage that the real work gets done, where the writing takes shape and begins to emerge in its final form. Most professional writers spend much more time revising than they do writing the first draft. Don't skimp on this part of the process or try to race through it.

It is a good idea not to start a major revision the minute a draft is complete. Take a break. Exercise, have a meal, do something completely different to clear your mind. If possible, put the draft aside for at least a day, so that when you return to it you'll have a fresh perspective and can begin truly reseeing it. Print out your draft. Attempting serious revision on-screen is generally a bad idea—we see differently, and we usually see more, when we read off a printed page. Read with a pen in your hand and annotate your text just the way you would a piece of literature, looking for the strengths and weaknesses of your argument. The process laid out here consists of three phases: *global revisions*, or large-scale revisions; *local revisions*, or small-scale revisions; and the final *editing and proofreading*. If you haven't done so before, revising your paper three times may seem like a lot of work, but bear in mind that most professional writers revise their work many more times than that. Revision is the real key to writing the best paper you can.

Global Revision

On a first pass at revision—the large-scale, global part of the process—don't worry too much about details like word choice, punctuation, and so forth. Too many students focus so much on these issues that they miss the big picture. The details are important, but you will deal with them in depth later. You wouldn't want to spend your time getting the wording of a sentence just right only to decide later that the paragraph it is in weakens your argument and needs to be deleted. So at first, look at the overall picture—the argument, organization, and tone of the paper as a whole. While there's nothing wrong with making a few small improvements as you read, nothing smaller than a paragraph should concern you at this point. Here are some possibilities for how you might revise your paper globally.

GLOBAL REVISION CHECKLIST

Further develop your focus and thesis.

☐ Can your reader immediately identify what the topic of the essay will be—that is, which text(s), and which aspect of the text (for example, character development or the use of particular language features), you will analyze?

☐ Have you narrowed the scope of the thesis for your reader? How could it be further narrowed? Remember, it's not enough to say "Women are portrayed differently in *X* and *Y*." What do you mean by "differently"?

☐ Have you answered the larger "So what?" question? What is at stake in your thesis, and why will it matter to your readers?

Reorganize your paper, if necessary.

☐ Does each of your topic sentences provide a strong transition from one paragraph to the next? Does the order of the ideas and paragraphs make immediate sense to you, or does some alternate structure suggest itself?

Expand your paper with new paragraphs or with new evidence within existing paragraphs.

☐ What textual evidence have you used? Is it sufficiently provocative and persuasive?

☐ Have you successfully integrated quotations, summaries, or paraphrases into your own writing, while at the same time acknowledging your source?

Eliminate any unnecessary, contradictory, or distracting passages.

☐ Does every piece of evidence, every sentence, and every paragraph contribute to the validity of your argument?

Clarify difficult passages with more specific explanations or evidence.

☐ Have you worked to convey why you are citing a particular passage? What *particular* details in it provide evidence that supports your interpretation?

Once you have completed your first, large-scale revision, chances are you will feel more confident about the content and structure of your paper. The thesis and focus are strong, the evidence is lined up, and the major points are clear. Print out the new version, take another break if you can, and prepare to move on to the second phase of revision, the one that takes place at the local level of words, phrases, and sentences.

Local Revision

The focus here is on style and clarity. The types of changes you will make in this stage are, essentially, small-scale versions of the changes you made in the first round of revision: adding, cutting, reorganizing, and clarifying.

LOCAL REVISION CHECKLIST

Consider your sentences.

☐ Do you use a variety of sentence types and sentences of different lengths to sustain the interest of your reader?

☐ Does each sentence clearly follow from the last one, or do you need to reorganize the sentences within a particular paragraph to provide clearer transitions between sentences?

☐ Look at the first and last sentences in each paragraph. Do they provide sufficient transitions from one paragraph to the next?

Consider your word choice.

☐ Do you use the same words and phrases again and again? If so, could you vary your word choice a bit?

☐ If you use any special literary terms, are you absolutely certain that you are using these terms correctly?

☐ Take a look at the verbs. Are many of them strong and active, or do most sentences rely on dull linking verbs like *is* or *seems*?

Final Editing and Proofreading

Once you have revised your essay a second time and achieved both content and a style that please you, it's time for a final edit. This is where you make it "correct."

FINAL EDITING CHECKLIST

Check your spelling.

☐ Have you spelled everything correctly? (Should it be *their* or *there*? Should it be *it's* or *its*?) Do not rely on your computer's spell-check function. This only tells you if the word you typed is a word, not if it's the correct word. When in doubt, look it up.

Check your punctuation.

☐ Look for things that have caused you trouble in the past. Should you use a comma or a semicolon? Again, when in doubt, look it up.

☐ Pay special attention to quotations. Does the question mark go inside or outside the quotation marks? Have you used both opening and closing quotation marks for each quotation?

Check your formatting.

☐ Is your manuscript format correct? Unless your instructor has provided other instructions, follow the format described on pages 50–51.

☐ Have you italicized or underlined titles of plays and novels (*Othello*) and put the titles of short stories and poems in quotation marks ("Hills Like White Elephants"; "I heard a Fly buzz—when I died")?

☐ Does your Works Cited list follow MLA format, and do you properly cite your quotations in the body of the text? Nobody expects you to know all the rules on your own, but you should know where to look for them.

☐ If you have questions about citation and formatting, look them up in this book or in a good dictionary, grammar handbook, or other reference.

Here is a paragraph ready for final editing from a student essay on *Hamlet*. Notice the kinds of corrections that the student will have to make before the paragraph is done.

The supernatural relm affects the revenge tragedy in other ways than the appearance and presence of ghosts. In Hamlet, the religious concern with final absolution both inflames Hamlet's desire for revenge and causes him to hesitate in carrying out revenge. Not only has Hamlet's father been murdered, but he was also Cut off even in the blossoms of [his] sin, / Unhousled, disappointed, unanel'd, / No reck'ning made, but sent to [his] account / With all [his] imperfections on [his] head (1.5.77–80). For Hamlet's father, being murdered is doubly disastrous; not only is his life cut short. But he must burn away "the foul crimes done in [his] days of nature" in purgatory before he can be granted access to heaven (1.5.13). A normal death would have afforded him final absolution, and thus a direct route to heaven. The same concern that makes Hamlet's father's death even more terrible also causes Hamlet to pass on a perfect opportunity to exact revenge on his father's murderer. Hamlet finds Claudius praying, alone. To kill a man in prayer means to kill a man who has had all his sins absolved. Hamlet observes Claudius and reasons: "A villain kills my father, and for that, / I, his sole son, do this same villain send / To heaven." (3.3.76–78) Hamlet's concern for the supernatural afterlife affects his carrying out revenge.

Spelling: "realm"

Italicize "Hamlet."

Remember to add quotation marks around the direct quotation.

This should be a comma joining two sentence fragments.

This period belongs outside the parentheses, after the act, scene, and line number.

One final word of advice as you revise your paper—ask for help. Doing so is neither cheating nor an admission of defeat. In fact, professional writers do it all the time. Despite the persistent image of writers toiling in isolation, most successful writers seek advice at various stages. More important, they are willing to listen to that advice and to rethink what they have written if it seems not to be communicating what they had intended.

PEER EDITING AND WORKSHOPS

Some instructors give class time for draft workshops, sometimes called *peer editing*, in which you work with your fellow students, trying to help one another improve your work-in-progress. Such workshops can benefit you in two ways. First, your classmates can offer you critiques and advice on what you might have missed in your own rereading. Second, reading and discussing papers other than your own will help you grow as a writer, showing you a variety of ways in which a topic can be approached. If you really like something about a peer's paper—say, a vivid introduction or the effective use of humor—make note of how it works within the paper and consider integrating something similar into a future paper of your own. We are not, of course, advocating copying your classmates; rather, we are pointing out that you can learn a lot from other people's writing.

Your instructor may give you guidelines regarding what to look for in others' drafts, or you may be left more or less on your own. In either case, keep these general guidelines in mind:

- **Be respectful of one another's work.** You should, of course, treat your peers' work with the same respect and seriousness that you would want for your own. Keep your criticism constructive and avoid personal attacks, even if you disagree strongly with an opinion. You can help your fellow writers by expressing a contrary opinion in a civilized and thoughtful manner.

- **Be honest.** This means giving real, constructive criticism when it is due. Don't try to spare your workshop partner's feelings by saying, "That's great," or, "It's fine," when it really isn't. When asked what went badly in a peer workshop, students most commonly respond *not* that their peers were too harsh on their work but that they were not harsh enough. Wouldn't you rather hear about a problem with your work from a peer in a draft workshop than from your professor after you have already handed in the final draft? So would your classmates.

- **Look for the good as well as the bad in a draft.** No paper, no matter how rough or problematic, is completely without merit. And no paper, no matter how clever or well written, couldn't be improved. By pointing out both what works and what doesn't, you will help your classmates grow as writers.

- **Keep an eye on the time.** It's easy to get wrapped up in a discussion of an interesting paper and not allow adequate time for another paper. Say you're given half an hour to work with your draft and that of one classmate. When you reach the fifteen-minute mark, move on, no matter how interesting your discussion is. Fair is fair. On the other hand, don't stop short of the allotted time. If you are reading carefully and thinking hard about one another's drafts, it should be impossible to finish early.

- **Take notes on your draft itself or on a separate sheet.** You may be certain that you will remember what was said in a workshop, but you would be amazed how often people forget the good advice they heard and intended to follow. Better safe than sorry — take careful notes.

- **Ask questions.** Asking questions about portions of a draft you don't understand or find problematic can help its writer see what needs to be clarified, expanded, or reworked. Useful questions can range from large (*What is the purpose of this paragraph?*) to small (*Is this a quote? Who said it?*) in size.

- **Don't assume that explaining yourself to your workshop partner can replace revision.** Sometimes your workshop partners will ask a question, and when you answer it for them, they will say, "Oh, right, that makes sense," leaving you with the impression that everything is clear now. But remember, your classmates didn't understand it from the writing alone, and you won't be there to explain it to your instructor.

- **Be specific in your comments.** Vague comments like, "The introduction is good," or, "It's sort of confusing here," are not much help. Aim for something more like, "The introduction was funny and really made me want to read on," or, "This paragraph confused me because it seems to contradict what you said in the previous one." With comments like these, a writer will have a much better sense of where to focus his or her revision energies.

- **Try to focus on the big picture.** When you are reading a draft, it's tempting to zero in on distracting little mistakes in spelling, punctuation, or word choice. While it's generally fine to point out or circle such surface matters as you go along, a draft workshop is not about correcting mistakes. It's about helping one another to resee and rethink your papers on a global scale.

- **Push your partners to help you more.** If your workshop partners seem shy or reluctant to criticize, prompt them to say more by letting them know that you really want advice and that you are able to take criticism. Point out to them what you perceive as the trouble spots in the essay, and ask if they have any ideas to help you out.

It feels good, of course, to hear that someone likes your paper and cannot imagine how to improve it. But in the long run it is even better to get real, useful advice that will lead to a better paper. If your classmates are not helping you enough, it's your responsibility to ask for more criticism.

Even if your class does not include workshop time, you can still use the many resources available to you on campus. Find one or two other members of your class and conduct your own peer workshop, reading and critiquing one another's drafts. Be sure to arrange such a meeting far enough in advance of the due date so that you will have ample time to implement any good revision advice you receive. Many campuses also have writing or tutoring centers, and the tutors in these centers, often advanced students who are skilled writers, can offer a good deal of help. Remember, again, that you should make an appointment to see a tutor well in advance of the paper's due date, and you should *not* expect a tutor or mentor to revise or "fix" your paper for you. That is, ultimately, your job. And, of course, you can also approach your instructor at any phase of the writing process and ask for advice and help.

But remember, no matter where you turn for advice, the final responsibility for your paper is yours. Any advice and help you receive from classmates, tutors, friends — or even your instructor — is just that: advice and help. It is *your* paper, and *you* must be the one to make the decisions about which advice to follow and which to ignore, and how to implement changes to improve your paper. The key is to keep an open mind, seek help from all available sources, and give yourself plenty of time to turn your first draft into a final paper that makes you truly proud.

TIPS FOR WRITING ABOUT LITERATURE

Each genre of literature — fiction, poetry, and drama — poses its own, slightly different set of assumptions, opportunities, and problems for writers, which are covered in more detail in the sections that follow. However, the following general principles can help you as you write about any form of literature:

- **Don't assume that your readers will remember (or consider important) the same ideas or incidents in the literature that you do.** You should assume that your readers have *read* the literature but not necessarily that they have reacted to it the same way you have. Therefore, whenever possible, use specific examples and evidence in the form of quotations and summaries to back up your claims.

- **Do not retell the plot or text at length.** Some writers are tempted to begin with a plot summary or even to include the text of a short poem at the beginning of a paper. However, this strategy can backfire by delaying the real substance of your paper. Be discriminating when you summarize—keep quotations short and get to the point you want to make as quickly as possible.

- **Do not assume that quotations or summaries are self-sufficient and prove your point automatically.** Summaries and quotations are a starting point; you need to analyze them thoroughly in your own words, explaining why they are important. As a general rule, each quotation or summary should be followed by at least several sentences of analysis.

- **It is customary to use the present tense when writing about literature,** even if the events discussed take place in the distant past.

  When she sees that Romeo is dead, Juliet kills herself with his knife.

- **The first time you mention an author, use his or her full name.** For subsequent references, the last name is sufficient. (Do not use first names only; it sounds as if you know an author personally.)

- **Titles of poems, short stories, and essays should be put in quotation marks. Titles of books, plays, and periodicals (magazines, newspapers, and so forth) should be italicized or underlined.** In titles and in all quotations, follow spelling, capitalization, and punctuation exactly as it occurs in the work itself.

- **Give your paper a title.** A title doesn't need to be elaborate or super clever, but it should give some clue to your readers as to what the paper is about and begin setting up their expectations. Simply restating the assignment, such as "Essay #2" or "Comparison and Contrast Paper," is of little help to a reader and might even suggest intellectual laziness on your part. For the same reason, avoid giving your paper the same title as the work of literature you are writing about; unless you're Shakespeare or Hemingway, don't title your paper *Hamlet* or "A Clean, Well-Lighted Place."

- **Above all, use common sense and *be consistent*.**

USING QUOTATIONS EFFECTIVELY

At some point, you will want to quote the literature you are citing, and you might also want to quote some secondary research sources as well. Quotations ground your paper in the literature you are discussing and prevent your argument from being overly abstract. They also allow the author of the literature a chance to shine through in his or her own words, showing that you respect and appreciate the author's work. Quotations bring emphasis, variety, and specificity to your writing. Be selective, though, in your use of quotations so that the dominant voice of the paper is your own, not a patchwork of the words of others. Here is general advice to help you integrate quotations effectively into your essays.

Avoiding Floating Quotations

Try to avoid floating quotations. Sometimes writers simply lift a sentence out of the original, put quotation marks around it, and identify the source (if at all) in a subsequent sentence. Doing so can create confusion for a reader, who is momentarily left to ponder where the quotation comes from and why have you quoted it. In addition to potentially causing confusion, such quoting can read as awkward and choppy, as there is no transition between another writer's words and yours.

Use at least an attributed quotation — that is, one that names the source *within* the sentence containing the quotation, usually in a lead-in phrase. This way the reader knows right away who originally wrote or said the quoted material and knows (or at least expects) that your commentary will follow. It also provides a smoother transition between your words and the quotation.

Problem: Floating Quotation	Solution: Use a Lead-in Phrase
"I met a traveler from an antique land." This is how Shelley's poem "Ozymandias" begins.	**Shelley begins his poem** "Ozymandias" **with the words** "I met a traveler from an antique land."

Integrating Quotations

Whenever possible, use an integrated quotation. To do this, make the quotation a part of your own sentence, as shown in the lead-in phrase in the table above. This is the hardest sort of quoting to do since it requires that you make the quoted material fit in grammatically with your own sentence, but the payoff in clarity and sharp prose is usually well worth the extra time spent on sentence revision.

Adding to or Altering a Quotation

Sometimes, especially when you are using integrated quotations effectively, you will find that you need to slightly alter the words you are quoting. You should, of course, keep quotations exact whenever possible, but occasionally the disparity between the tense, point of view, or grammar of your sentence and that of the quoted material will necessitate some alterations. Other difficulties can arise when you quote a passage that already contains a quotation or when you need to combine quotation marks with other punctuation marks. When any of these situations arise, the following guidelines should prove useful. The following examples of quoted text are all drawn from this original passage from *Hamlet*, specifically the scene in which Hamlet and his friend Horatio are watching a gravedigger unearth old skulls in a cemetery:

> HAMLET: That skull had a tongue in it, and could sing once. How the knave jowls it to the ground, as if 'twere Cain's jaw-bone, that did the first murder! This might be the pate of a politician, which this ass now o'erreaches, one that would circumvent God, might it not?
> HORATIO: It might, my lord.
> HAMLET: Or of a courtier, which could say "Good morrow, sweet lord! How dost thou, sweet lord?" This might be my Lord Such-a-one, that prais'd my Lord Such-a-one's horse when 'a meant to beg it, might it not? (5.1.70–80)

If you ever alter anything in a quotation or add words to it in order to make it clear and grammatically consistent with your own writing, you need to signal to your readers what you have added or changed. This is done by enclosing your words within square brackets in order to distinguish them from those in the source. If, for instance, you feel Hamlet's reference to the gravedigger as "this ass" is unclear, you could clarify it either by substituting your own words, as in the first example below, or by adding the identifying phrase to the original quote, as in the second example:

> Hamlet wonders if it is "the pate of a politician, which [the gravedigger] now o'erreaches" (5.1.73–74).

> Hamlet wonders if it is "the pate of a politician, which this ass [the gravedigger] now o'erreaches" (5.1.73–74).

Omitting Words from a Quotation

To keep a quotation focused, you will sometimes want to omit words, phrases, or even whole sentences that do not contribute to your point. Any omission is signaled by ellipses, or three spaced periods, with square brackets around them. (The brackets are required to distinguish your own ellipses from any that might occur in the original source.)

> Hamlet wonders if the skull "might be the pate of a politician [. . .] that would circumvent God" (5.1.73–74).

It is usually not necessary to use ellipses at the beginning of a quotation, since a reader assumes you are quoting only a relevant portion of text, but MLA style recommends using ellipses at the end of a quotation if words are dropped at the end of the final quoted sentence.

Quotations within Quotations

If you are quoting material that itself contains a quotation, the internal quotation is set off with single quotation marks rather than the standard double quotation marks that will enclose the entire quotation.

> Hamlet wonders if he might be looking at the skull "of a courtier, which could say 'Good morrow, sweet lord! How dost thou, sweet lord?'" (5.1.76–77).

When the text you're quoting contains *only* material already in quotation marks in the original, the standard double quotation marks are all you need.

> Hamlet wonders if the courtier once said, "Good morrow, sweet lord! How dost thou, sweet lord?" (5.1.76–77).

Quotation Marks with Other Punctuation

When a period or a comma comes at the end of a quotation, it should always be placed inside the closing quotation marks, except when the quotation is followed by a parenthetical in-text citation, as shown below. In this case the period should follow the parenthesis.

> Hamlet muses that the skull might have belonged to "my Lord Such-a-one, that prais'd my Lord Such-a-one's horse" (5.1.78–79).

In this next example, the comma following "once" is also within the quotation marks, even though in Shakespeare's original "once" is followed by a period.

> "That skull had a tongue in it, and could sing once," muses Hamlet.

Question marks and exclamation points are placed inside the quotation marks if they are part of the original quotation and outside the marks if they are part of your own sentence but not part of the passage you are quoting. In this first example, the question is Hamlet's, and so the question mark must be placed within the quotation marks.

> Hamlet asks Horatio if the skull "might be my Lord Such-a-one, that prais'd my Lord Such-a-one's horse when 'a meant to beg it, might it not?" (5.1.78–79).

In this second example, the question is the essay writer's, and so the question mark is placed outside the quotation marks.

> Why is Hamlet so disturbed that this skull "might be the pate of a politician"? (5.1.73)

These sorts of punctuation details are notoriously hard to remember, so you should not feel discouraged if you begin forgetting such highly specialized rules moments after reading them. At least know where you can look them up, and do so when you proofread your paper. A willingness to attend to detail is what distinguishes serious students and gives writing a polished, professional appearance. Also, the more you work with quotations, the easier it will be to remember the rules.

QUOTING FROM STORIES

The guidelines that follow should be used not only when you quote from stories, but also for when you quote from any prose work, be it fiction or nonfiction.

Short Quotations

For short quotations of four lines or fewer, run the quotation in with your own text using quotation marks to signal the beginning and the end of the quotation.

> Young Goodman Brown notices that the branches touched by his companion "became strangely withered and dried up, as with a week's sunshine."

Long Quotations

When a quotation is longer than four lines in your text, set it off from your essay by beginning a new line and indenting it one inch from the left margin only, as shown here. This is called a block quotation:

> Young Goodman Brown then notices something strange about his companion:
>
> > As they went, he plucked a branch of maple to serve for a walking stick, and began to strip it of the twigs and little boughs, which were wet with evening dew. The moment his fingers touched them they became strangely withered and dried up, as with a week's sunshine. Thus the pair proceeded, . . ., until suddenly, . . . Goodman Brown sat himself down on the stump of a tree and refused to go any farther. (9)

Note that no quotation marks are used with block quotations. The indentation is sufficient to signal to your readers that this is a quotation.

QUOTING FROM POEMS

Short Quotations

For quotations of up to three lines, run the text right into your own, using quotation marks just as you would with a prose quotation. However, since the placement of line endings can be significant in a poem, you need to indicate where they occur. This is done by including a slash mark, with a single space on each side, where the line breaks occur.

(Some students find this awkward-looking at first, but you will quickly get used to it. Your instructor will expect you to honor the poet's choices regarding line breaks.):

> In "Sailing to Byzantium," Yeats describes an old man as "a paltry thing, / A tattered coat upon a stick" (lines 9–10).

Long Quotations

For quotations of four lines or more, "block" the material, setting it off a half an inch from the left margin, duplicating all line breaks of the original. Do not use quotation marks with block quotations:

> In the very first stanza of "The Lake Isle of Innisfree," Yeats expresses a desire to return to a simple country life:
>
> > I will arise and go now, and go to Innisfree,
> > And a small cabin build there, of clay and wattles made:
> > Nine bean-rows will I have there, a hive for the honey-bee,
> > And live alone in the bee-loud glade.

QUOTING FROM PLAYS

Short Single-Speaker Passages

When you quote a short passage of drama with a single speaker, treat the quoted text just as you would prose fiction:

> Nora's first words in *A Doll House* are "Hide the Christmas Tree carefully, Helen. Be sure the children do not see it until this evening, when it is dressed."

Longer or More Complex Passages

For a longer quotation, or a quotation of any length involving more than one character, you will need to block off the quotation. Begin each separate piece of dialogue indented a half an inch from the left margin with the character's name, typed in capital letters, followed by a period. Subsequent lines of the character's speech should be indented an additional a quarter of an inch. (Your word processor's "hanging indent" function is useful for achieving this effect without having to indent each separate line.) As with fiction or poetry, do not use quotation marks for block quotations:

We see the tension between Nora and her husband in their very first confrontation:

> NORA. "Yes but, Torvald, this year we really can let ourselves go a little. This is the first Christmas that we have not needed to economise."
> HELMER. "Still, you know, we can't spend money recklessly."
> NORA. "Yes, Torvald, we may be a wee bit more reckless now, mayn't we?" (1.1)

Verse Drama

Many older plays, including classical Greek drama and much of the work of Shakespeare and his contemporaries, are written at least partly in poetic verse. When you quote a verse drama, you must respect the line endings, just as you do in quoting poetry. The example below shows a short quotation with slash marks that indicate line endings:

> Hamlet's most famous soliloquy begins, "To be, or not to be, that is the question: / Whether 'tis nobler in the mind to suffer / The slings and arrows of outrageous fortune" (3.1.56–58).

This second example shows a longer, block quotation in verse form:

> Hamlet then begins his most famous soliloquy:
>
> > To be, or not to be, that is the question:
> > Whether 'tis nobler in the mind to suffer
> > The slings and arrows of outrageous fortune,
> > Or to take arms against a sea of troubles,
> > And by opposing end them. (3.1.56–60)

Tips for Quoting

- **Double-check the wording, spelling, and punctuation of every quotation you use.** Even if something seems "wrong" in the original source—a nonstandard spelling, a strange mark of punctuation, or even a factual error—resist the urge to correct it. When you put quotation marks around something, you indicate that you are reproducing it exactly as it first appeared.
- **Use the shortest quotation you can while still making your point.** Remember, the focus should always be on your own ideas, and the dominant voice should be yours. Don't quote a paragraph

from a source when a single sentence contains the heart of what you need. Don't quote a whole sentence when you can simply integrate a few words into one of your own sentences.

- **Never assume a quotation is self-explanatory.** Each time you include a quotation, introduce it, analyze it, and explain why you have quoted it. Remember that your reader may have a different reaction to the quotation than you did.

- **If you are quoting a *character* in a story, play, or poem, be sure to distinguish that character from the *author*.** Hamlet says, "To be or not to be," not Shakespeare, and you should make that distinction clear.

- **Take care not to distort the meaning of a quotation.** It is intellectually dishonest to quote an author or a speaker out of context or to use ellipses or additions in such a way as to change the meaning or integrity of source material. Treat your sources with the same respect you would want if you were to be quoted in a newspaper or magazine.

FORMATTING YOUR PAPER

If your instructor gives you directions about what your paper should look like, follow them exactly. If not, the following basic guidelines on format, recommended by the Modern Language Association of America (MLA), will work well in most instances. The most comprehensive guide to MLA style is *MLA Handbook*, 8th Edition (2016). The guiding principle here is readability—you want the look of your paper to distract as little as possible from the content.

- **Use plain white paper, black ink, and a standard, easy-to-read font.** To make your paper stand out from the masses, it might seem like a nice touch to use visual design elements like colored or decorated paper, fancy fonts, and so forth. However, your instructor has a lot of reading to do, and anything that distracts or slows down that reading is a minus, not a plus, for your paper. For the same reason, avoid illustrations, pictures of authors, and so forth, unless they are needed to clarify a point. Distinguish your paper through content and style, not flashy design.

- **Include vital information in the upper-left corner of your first page.** This information usually consists of your name, the name of your instructor, the course number of the class, and the date you submit the paper.

- **Center your paper's title.** The title should appear in uppercase and lowercase letters, and in the same font as the rest of your paper—not italicized, boldface, or set within quotation marks.

- **Page numbers should appear in the upper-right corner of each page.** Do not include the word *page* or the abbreviation *p.* with the page numbers. Use your word processing program's "header" (or "running head") feature to include your last name before the page numbers.

See the sample student papers in this book for examples of correct MLA-style formatting. These basic guidelines should carry you through most situations, but if you have any questions regarding format, ask your instructor for his or her preferences.

CHAPTER 4

Common Writing Assignments

Chances are you will encounter a variety of writing assignments in your literature class, possibly ranging from a brief personal response to an extended literary research paper. Each assignment offers you two opportunities. First, writing about a particular piece (or multiple pieces) of literature forces you to think more closely than a simple reading does, so you will end up learning more about the story, poem, or play. Second, writing is your best opportunity to share your thoughts with your instructor, and possibly your classmates, so you can have an impact on someone else's thinking as well. Each time you get a new assignment, ask yourself, "What did I learn from the last assignment that I might apply to this one?" This chapter outlines some of the assignments you might be given (summary, response, explication, analysis, comparison and contrast, and essay exams), provides examples of each, and demonstrates how each skill might build on the previous skill.

SUMMARY

A **summary** is a brief recap of the most important points—plot, character, and so on—in a work of literature. To demonstrate that you have understood a story or play, for instance, you may be asked to summarize its plot as homework before class discussions. A summary of Nathaniel Hawthorne's "Young Goodman Brown" follows:

> Set in seventeenth-century Salem, Massachusetts, Nathaniel Hawthorne's "Young Goodman Brown" follows the fortunes of the title character when he leaves his young wife, Faith, for a mysterious rendezvous in a forest at night. The character he meets in the forbidding woods is unnamed, but Hawthorne hints that he may be the Devil himself. As they proceed deeper into the forest on their unspecified but presumably unholy errand, Goodman Brown's misgivings increase, especially when they encounter his fellow townsfolk—people Goodman Brown thought were good Christians—en route to the same meeting. But when they are joined by Faith, Brown recklessly resolves to participate. At the ceremony, the new converts are called forth, but as he and Faith step forward to be anointed in blood, he rebels and urges Faith to resist. Instantly he finds himself alone in the forest,

and when he returns to town the next morning, uncertain whether it was all a dream, he finds himself suspicious and wary of his neighbors and his wife. His "Faith" has been corrupted, and to the end of his days he remains a bitter and untrusting man: "his dying hour was gloom."

A summary can be longer or shorter than the above example, depending on your purpose. Notice that interpretation is kept to a minimum ("His 'Faith' has been corrupted") and the summary is recounted in the present tense ("he returns to town"; "he remains a bitter and untrusting man").

While a *summary* is not a kind of writing assignment that you will likely have to produce often in a literature course, *summarizing* is a skill you will need to develop. It is useful to be able to focus on the most important parts of a text, knowing what is most vital. Short summaries, either of a work (or part of a work) of literature or of critical essays about literature, are commonly used as part of the supporting evidence in more complex papers. When you are using secondary sources in a paper about a literary work—as when you write a literary research paper—chances are that your audience has not read the critical essays you have read. Therefore, you may need to briefly summarize for your readers the arguments of those critical essays. Ask yourself, "What do my readers need to know to follow my argument, and what evidence do I need to provide to convince them of my point of view?" Summarize accordingly.

RESPONSE

The goal of a response paper is twofold: 1) to describe your personal response to a particular reading assignment, and 2) to explain why you had this reaction. Of course, our reactions to literature are often multiple and complex, so you need to be selective in what you write. Don't try to explain every response and every thought you had while reading. Rather, choose one significant thought you had while reading and explore that in depth.

Response papers in general are somewhat informal and do not necessarily follow the thesis-and-support model common in other types of literature papers. Response papers are often fairly brief, and since you are writing about your personal responses, it's generally OK to use the first-person pronoun *I*. Remember, though, that this is not simply a personal essay in which you explore your own life and thoughts. Keep the literature as the main focus. Since there are no hard-and-fast rules about response papers, be sure to read your instructor's directions carefully and follow them closely.

After reading Zora Neale Hurston's short story "Sweat," which follows, take a moment to consider your own response to it and where that response comes from. Then read and consider the student response paper that follows.

ZORA NEALE HURSTON [1891–1960]

Sweat

It was eleven o'clock of a Spring night in Florida. It was Sunday. Any other night, Delia Jones would have been in bed for two hours by this time. But she was a washwoman, and Monday morning meant a great deal to her. So she collected the soiled clothes on Saturday when she returned the clean things. Sunday night after church, she sorted them and put the white things to soak. It saved her almost a half day's start. A great hamper in the bedroom held the clothes that she brought home. It was so much neater than a number of bundles lying around.

She squatted in the kitchen floor beside the great pile of clothes, sorting them into small heaps according to color, and humming a song in a mournful key, but wondering through it all where Sykes, her husband, had gone with her horse and buckboard.

Just then something long, round, limp, and black fell upon her shoulders and slithered to the floor beside her. A great terror took hold of her. It softened her knees and dried her mouth so that it was a full minute before she could cry out or move. Then she saw that it was the big bull whip her husband liked to carry when he drove.

She lifted her eyes to the door and saw him standing there bent over with laughter at her fright. She screamed at him.

"Sykes, what you throw dat whip on me like dat? You know it would skeer me—looks just like a snake, an' you knows how skeered Ah is of snakes."

"Course Ah knowed it! That's how come Ah done it." He slapped his leg with his hand and almost rolled on the ground in his mirth. "If you such a big fool dat you got to have a fit over a earth worm or a string, Ah don't keer how bad Ah skeer you."

"You aint got no business doing it. Gawd knows it's a sin. Some day Ah'm gointuh drop dead from some of yo' foolishness. 'Nother thing, where you been wid mah rig? Ah feeds dat pony. He aint fuh you to be drivin' wid no bull whip."

"You sho is one aggravatin' nigger woman!" he declared and stepped into the room. She resumed her work and did not answer him at once.

54

"Ah done tole you time and again to keep them white folks' clothes outa dis house."

He picked up the whip and glared down at her. Delia went on with her work. She went out into the yard and returned with a galvanized tub and sat it on the washbench. She saw that Sykes had kicked all of the clothes together again, and now stood in her way truculently, his whole manner hoping, *praying*, for an argument. But she walked calmly around him and commenced to re-sort the things.

"Next time, Ah'm gointer kick 'em outdoors," he threatened as he struck a match along the leg of his corduroy breeches.

Delia never looked up from her work, and her thin, stooped shoulders sagged further.

"Ah aint for no fuss t'night, Sykes. Ah just come from taking sacrament at the church house."

He snorted scornfully. "Yeah, you just come from de church house on a Sunday night, but heah you is gone to work on them clothes. You ain't nothing but a hypocrite. One of them amen-corner Christians—sing, whoop, and shout, then come home and wash white folks clothes on the Sabbath."

He stepped roughly upon the whitest pile of things, kicking them helter-skelter as he crossed the room. His wife gave a little scream of dismay, and quickly gathered them together again.

"Sykes, you quit grindin' dirt into these clothes! How can Ah git through by Sat'day if Ah don't start on Sunday?"

"Ah don't keer if you never git through. Anyhow, Ah done promised Gawd and a couple of other men, Ah aint gointer have it in mah house. Don't gimme no lip neither, else Ah'll throw 'em out and put mah fist up side yo' head to boot."

Delia's habitual meekness seemed to slip from her shoulders like a blown scarf. She was on her feet; her poor little body, her bare knuckly hands bravely defying the strapping hulk before her.

"Looka heah, Sykes, you done gone too fur. Ah been married to you fur fifteen years, and Ah been takin' in washin' fur fifteen years. Sweat, sweat, sweat! Work and sweat, cry and sweat, pray and sweat!"

"What's that got to do with me?" he asked brutally.

"What's it got to do with you, Sykes? Mah tub of suds is filled yo' belly with vittles more times than yo' hands is filled it. Mah sweat is done paid for this house and Ah reckon Ah kin keep on sweatin' in it."

She seized the iron skillet from the stove and struck a defensive pose, which act surprised him greatly, coming from her. It cowed him and he did not strike her as he usually did.

"Naw you won't," she panted, "that ole snaggle-toothed black woman you runnin' with aint comin' heah to pile up on *mah* sweat and blood.

You aint paid for nothin' on this place, and Ah'm gointer stay right heah till Ah'm toted out foot foremost."

"Well, you better quit gittin' me riled up, else they'll be totin' you out sooner than you expect. Ah'm so tired of you Ah don't know whut to do. Gawd! how Ah hates skinny wimmen!"

A little awed by this new Delia, he sidled out of the door and slammed the back gate after him. He did not say where he had gone, but she knew too well. She knew very well that he would not return until nearly daybreak also. Her work over, she went on to bed but not to sleep at once. Things had come to a pretty pass!

She lay awake, gazing upon the debris that cluttered their matrimonial trail. Not an image left standing along the way. Anything like flowers had long ago been drowned in the salty stream that had been pressed from her heart. Her tears, her sweat, her blood. She had brought love to the union and he had brought a longing after the flesh. Two months after the wedding, he had given her the first brutal beating. She had the memory of his numerous trips to Orlando with all of his wages when he had returned to her penniless, even before the first year had passed. She was young and soft then, but now she thought of her knotty, muscled limbs, her harsh knuckly hands, and drew herself up into an unhappy little ball in the middle of the big feather bed. Too late now to hope for love, even if it were not Bertha it would be someone else. This case differed from the others only in that she was bolder than the others. Too late for everything except her little home. She had built it for her old days, and planted one by one the trees and flowers there. It was lovely to her, lovely.

Somehow, before sleep came, she found herself saying aloud: "Oh well, whatever goes over the Devil's back, is got to come under his belly. Sometime or ruther, Sykes, like everybody else, is gointer reap his sowing." After that she was able to build a spiritual earthworks against her husband. His shells could no longer reach her. *Amen*. She went to sleep and slept until he announced his presence in bed by kicking her feet and rudely snatching the cover away.

"Gimme some kivah heah, an' git yo' damn foots over on yo' own side! Ah oughter mash you in yo' mouf fuh drawing dat skillet on me."

Delia went clear to the rail without answering him. A triumphant indifference to all that he was or did.

The week was as full of work for Delia as all other weeks, and Saturday found her behind her little pony, collecting and delivering clothes.

It was a hot, hot day near the end of July. The village men on Joe Clarke's porch even chewed cane listlessly. They did not hurl the caneknots as usual. They let them dribble over the edge of the porch. Even conversation had collapsed under the heat.

"Heah come Delia Jones," Jim Merchant said, as the shaggy pony came 'round the bend of the road toward them. The rusty buckboard was heaped with baskets of crisp, clean laundry.

"Yep," Joe Lindsay agreed. "Hot or col', rain or shine, jes ez reg'lar ez de weeks roll roun' Delia carries 'em an' fetches 'em on Sat'day."

"She better if she wanter eat," said Moss. "Sykes Jones aint wuth de shot an' powder hit would tek tuh kill 'em. Not to *huh* he aint."

"He sho' aint," Walter Thomas chimed in. "It's too bad, too, cause she wuz a right pritty li'l trick when he got huh. Ah'd uh mah'ied huh mahseff if he hadnter beat me to it."

Delia nodded briefly at the men as she drove past.

"Too much knockin' will ruin *any* 'oman. He done beat huh 'nough tuh kill three women, let 'lone change they looks," said Elijah Moseley. "How Sykes kin stommuck dat big black greasy Mogul he's layin' roun' wid, gits me. Ah swear dat eight-rock couldn't kiss a sardine can Ah done thowed out de back do' 'way las' yeah."

"Aw, she's fat, thass how come. He's allus been crazy 'bout fat women," put in Merchant. "He'd a' been tied up wid one long time ago if he could a' found one tuh have him. Did Ah tell yuh 'bout im come sidlin' roun' *mah* wife—bringin' her a basket uh pee-cans outa his yard fuh a present? Yessir, mah wife! She tol' him tuh take 'em right straight back home, cause Delia works so hard ovah dat washtub she reckon eveything on de place taste lak sweat an' soapsuds. Ah jus' wisht Ah'd a' caught 'im 'roun' dere! Ah'd a' made his hips ketch on fiah down dat shell road."

"Ah know he done it, too. Ah sees 'im grinnin' at every 'oman dat passes," Walter Thomas said. "But even so, he useter eat some mighty big hunks uh humble pie tuh git dat lil' 'oman he got. She wuz ez pritty ez a speckled pup! Dat wuz fifteen yeahs ago. He useter be so skeered uh losin' huh, she could make him do some parts of a husband's duty. Dey never wuz de same in de mind."

"There oughter be a law about him," said Lindsay. "He aint fit tuh carry guts tuh a bear."

Clarke spoke for the first time. "Taint no law on earth dat kin make a man be decent if it aint in 'im. There's plenty men dat takes a wife lak dey do a joint uh sugar-cane. It's round, juicy an' sweet when dey gits it. But dey squeeze an' grind, squeeze an' grind an' wring tell dey wring every drop uh pleasure dat's in 'em out. When dey's satisfied dat dey is wrung dry, dey treats 'em jes lak dey do a cane-chew. Dey throws 'em away. Dey knows whut dey is doin' while dey is at it, an' hates theirselves fuh it but they keeps on hangin' after huh tell she's empty. Den dey hates huh fuh bein' a cane-chew an' in de way."

"We oughter take Sykes an' dat stray 'oman uh his'n down in Lake Howell swamp an' lay on de rawhide till they cain't say 'Lawd a' mussy.'

He allus wuz uh ovahbearin' niggah, but since dat white 'oman from up north done teached 'im how to run a automobile, he done got too big-gety to live—an' we oughter kill 'im," Old Man Anderson advised.

A grunt of approval went around the porch. But the heat was melting their civic virtue and Elijah Moseley began to bait Joe Clarke.

"Come on, Joe, git a melon outa dere an' slice it up for yo' customers. We'se all sufferin' wid de heat. De bear's done got *me!*"

"Thass right, Joe, a watermelon is jes' whut Ah needs tuh cure de eppizudicks." Walter Thomas joined forces with Moseley. "Come on dere, Joe. We all is steady customers an' you aint set us up in a long time. Ah chooses dat long, bowlegged Floridy favorite."

"A god, an' be dough. You all gimme twenty cents and slice away," Clarke retorted. "Ah needs a col' slice m'self. Heah, everybody chip in. Ah'll lend y'all mah meat knife."

The money was quickly subscribed and the huge melon brought forth. At that moment, Sykes and Bertha arrived. A determined silence fell on the porch and the melon was put away again.

Merchant snapped down the blade of his jack-knife and moved toward the store door.

"Come on in, Joe, an' gimme a slab uh sow belly an' uh pound uh coffee—almost fuhgot 'twas Sat'day. Got to git on home." Most of the men left also.

Just then Delia drove past on her way home, as Sykes was ordering magnificently for Bertha. It pleased him for Delia to see.

"Git whutsoever yo' heart desires, Honey. Wait a minute, Joe. Give huh two botles uh strawberry soda-water, uh quart uh parched ground-peas, an a block uh chewin' gum."

With all this they left the store, with Sykes reminding Bertha that this was his town and she could have it if she wanted it.

The men returned soon after they left, and held their watermelon feast.

"Where did Sykes Jones git dat 'oman from nohow?" Lindsay asked.

"Ovah Apopka. Guess dey musta been cleanin' out de town when she lef'. She don't look lak a thing but a hunk uh liver wid hair on it."

"Well, she sho' kin squall," Dave Carter contributed. "When she gits ready tuh laff, she jes' opens huh mouf an' latches it back tuh de las' notch. No ole grandpa alligator down in Lake Bell aint got nothin' on huh."

Bertha had been in town three months now. Sykes was still paying her room rent at Della Lewis'—the only house in town that would have taken her in. Sykes took her frequently to Winter Park to "stomps." He still assured her that he was the swellest man in the state.

"Sho' you kin have dat lil' ole house soon's Ah kin git dat 'oman outa dere. Everything b'longs tuh me an' you sho' kin have it. Ah sho' 'bominates uh skinny 'oman. Lawdy, you sho' is got one portly shape on you! You kin git *anything* you wants. Dis is *mah* town an' you sho' kin have it."

Delia's work-worn knees crawled over the earth in Gethsemane and up the rocks of Calvary many, many times during these months. She avoided the villagers and meeting places in her efforts to be blind and deaf. But Bertha nullified this to a degree, by coming to Delia's house to call Sykes out to her at the gate.

Delia and Sykes fought all the time now with no peaceful interludes. They slept and ate in silence. Two or three times Delia had attempted a timid friendliness, but she was repulsed each time. It was plain that the breaches must remain agape.

The sun had burned July to August. The heat streamed down like a million hot arrows, smiting all things living upon the earth. Grass withered, leaves browned, snakes went blind in shedding, and men and dogs went mad. Dog days!

Delia came home one day and found Sykes there before her. She wondered, but started to go on into the house without speaking, even though he was standing in the kitchen door and she must either stoop under his arm or ask him to move. He made no room for her. She noticed a soap box beside the steps, but paid no particular attention to it, knowing that he must have brought it there. As she was stooping to pass under his outstretched arm, he suddenly pushed her backward, laughingly.

"Look in de box dere Delia, Ah done brung yuh somethin'!"

She nearly fell upon the box in her stumbling, and when she saw what it held, she all but fainted outright.

"Sykes! Sykes, mah Gawd! You take dat rattlesnake 'way from heah! You *gottuh*. Oh, Jesus, have mussy!"

"Ah aint gut tuh do nothin' uh de kin'—fact is Ah aint got tuh do nothin' but die. Taint no use uh you puttin' on airs makin' out lak you skeered uh dat snake—he's gointer stay right heah tell he die. He wouldn't bite me cause Ah knows how tuh handle 'im. Nohow he wouldn't risk breakin' out his fangs 'gin *yo'* skinny laigs."

"Naw, now Sykes, don't keep dat thing 'roun' heah tuh skeer me tuh death. You knows Ah'm even feared uh earth worms. Thass de biggest snake Ah evah did see. Kill 'im Sykes, please."

"Doan ast me tuh do nothin' fuh yuh. Goin' 'roun' tryin' tuh be so damn astorperious. Naw, Ah aint gonna kill it. Ah think uh damn sight mo' uh him dan you! Dat's a nice snake an' anybody doan lak 'im kin jes' hit de grit."

The village soon heard that Sykes had the snake, and came to see and ask questions.

"How de hen-fire did you ketch dat six-foot rattler, Sykes?" Thomas asked.

"He's full uh frogs so he caint hardly move, thass how Ah eased up on 'm. But Ah'm a snake charmer an' knows how tuh handle 'em. Shux, dat aint nothin'. Ah could ketch one eve'y day if Ah so wanted tuh."

"Whut he needs is a heavy hick'ry club leaned real heavy on his head. Dat's de bes 'way tuh charm a rattlesnake."

"Naw, Walt, y'all jes' don't understand dese diamon' backs lak Ah do," said Sykes in a superior tone of voice.

The village agreed with Walter, but the snake stayed on. His box remained by the kitchen door with its screen wire covering. Two or three days later it had digested its meal of frogs and literally came to life. It rattled at every movement in the kitchen or the yard. One day as Delia came down the kitchen steps she saw his chalky-white fangs curved like scimitars hung in the wire meshes. This time she did not run away with averted eyes as usual. She stood for a long time in the doorway in a red fury that grew bloodier for every second that she regarded the creature that was her torment.

That night she broached the subject as soon as Sykes sat down to the table.

"Sykes, Ah wants you tuh take dat snake 'way fum heah. You done starved me an' Ah put up widcher, you done beat me an Ah took dat, but you done kilt all mah insides bringin' dat varmint heah."

Sykes poured out a saucer full of coffee and drank it deliberately before he answered her.

"A whole lot Ah keer 'bout how you feels inside uh out. Dat snake aint goin' no damn wheah till Ah gits ready fuh 'im tuh go. So fur as beatin' is concerned, yuh aint took near all dat you gointer take ef yuh stay 'roun' *me*."

Delia pushed back her plate and got up from the table. "Ah hates you, Sykes," she said calmly. "Ah hates you tuh de same degree dat Ah useter love yuh. Ah done took an' took till mah belly is full up tuh mah neck. Dat's de reason Ah got mah letter fum de church an' moved mah membership tuh Woodbridge—so Ah don't haftuh take no sacrament wid yuh. Ah don't wantuh see yuh 'roun' me a-tall. Lay 'roun' wid dat 'oman all yuh wants tuh, but gwan 'way fum me an' mah house. Ah hates yuh lak uh suck-egg dog."

Sykes almost let the huge wad of corn bread and collard greens he was chewing fall out of his mouth in amazement. He had a hard time whipping himself up to the proper fury to try to answer Delia.

"Well, Ah'm glad you does hate me. Ah'm sho' tiahed uh you hangin' ontuh me. Ah don't want yuh. Look at yuh stringey ole neck! Yo' rawbony laigs an' arms is enough tuh cut uh man tuh death. You looks jes' lak de devvul's doll-baby tuh *me*. You cain't hate me no worse dan Ah hates you. Ah been hatin' *you* fuh years."

"Yo' ole black hide don't look lak nothin' tuh me, but uh passed uh wrinkled up rubber, wid yo' big ole yeahs flappin' on each side lak uh paih uh buzzard wings. Don't think Ah'm gointuh be run 'way fum mah house neither. Ah'm goin' tuh de white folks bout *you*, mah young man, de very nex' time you lay yo' han's on me. Mah cup is done run ovah." Delia said this with no signs of fear and Sykes departed from the house, threatening her, but made not the slightest move to carry out any of them.

That night he did not return at all, and the next day being Sunday, Delia was glad that she did not have to quarrel before she hitched up her pony and drove the four miles to Woodbridge.

She stayed to the night service—"love feast"—which was very warm and full of spirit. In the emotional winds her domestic trials were borne far and wide so that she sang as she drove homeward,

> *Jurden water, black an' col'*
> *Chills de body, not de soul*
> *An' Ah wantah cross Jurden in uh calm time.*

She came from the barn to the kitchen door and stopped.

"Whut's de mattah, ol' satan, you aint kickin' up yo' racket?" She addressed the snake's box. Complete silence. She went on into the house with a new hope in its birth struggles. Perhaps her threat to go to the white folks had frightened Sykes! Perhaps he was sorry! Fifteen years of misery and suppression had brought Delia to the place where she would hope *anything* that looked towards a way over or through her wall of inhibitions.

She felt in the match safe behind the stove at once for a match. There was only one there.

"Dat niggah wouldn't fetch nothin' heah tuh save his rotten neck, but he kin run thew whut Ah brings quick enough. Now he done toted off nigh on tuh haff uh box uh matches. He done had dat 'oman heah in mah house, too."

Nobody but a woman could tell how she knew this even before she struck the match. But she did and it put her into a new fury.

Presently she brought in the tubs to put the white things to soak. This time she decided she need not bring the hamper out of the bedroom; she would go in there and do the sorting. She picked up the pot-bellied lamp and went in. The room was small and the hamper stood hard by the foot of the white iron bed. She could sit and reach through the bedposts—resting as she worked.

"Ah wantah cross Jurden in uh calm time." She was singing again. The mood of the "love feast" had returned. She threw back the lid of the basket almost gaily. Then, moved by both horror and terror, she sprung back toward the door. *There lay the snake in the basket!* He moved sluggishly at first, but even as she turned round and round, jumped up and down in an insanity of fear, he began to stir vigorously. She saw him pouring his awful beauty from the basket upon the bed, then she seized the lamp and ran as fast as she could to the kitchen. The wind from the open door blew out the light and the darkness added to her terror. She sped to the darkness of the yard, slamming the door after her before she thought to set down the lamp. She did not feel safe even on the ground, so she climbed up in the hay barn.

There for an hour or more she lay sprawled upon the hay a gibbering wreck.

Finally she grew quiet, and after that, coherent thought. With this, stalked through her a cold, bloody rage. Hours of this. A period of introspection, a space of retrospection, then a mixture of both. Out of this an awful calm.

"Well, Ah done de bes' Ah could. If things aint right, Gawd knows taint mah fault."

She went to sleep—a twitchy sleep—and woke up to a faint gray sky. There was a loud hollow sound below. She peered out. Sykes was at the wood-pile, demolishing a wire-covered box.

He hurried to the kitchen door, but hung outside there some minutes before he entered, and stood some minutes more inside before he closed it after him.

The gray in the sky was spreading. Delia descended without fear now, and crouched beneath the low bedroom window. The drawn shade shut out the dawn, shut in the night. But the thin walls held back no sound.

"Dat ol' scratch is woke up now!" She mused at the tremendous whirr inside, which every woodsman knows, is one of the sound illusions. The rattler is a ventriloquist. His whirr sounds to the right, to the left, straight ahead, behind, close under foot—everywhere but where it is. Woe to him who guesses wrong unless he is prepared to hold up his end of the argument! Sometimes he strikes without rattling at all.

Inside, Sykes heard nothing until he knocked a pot lid off the stove while trying to reach the match safe in the dark. He had emptied his pockets at Bertha's.

The snake seemed to wake up under the stove and Sykes made a quick leap into the bedroom. In spite of the gin he had had, his head was clearing now.

"Mah Gawd!" he chattered, "ef Ah could on'y strack uh light!"

The rattling ceased for a moment as he stood paralyzed. He waited. It seemed that the snake waited also.

"Oh fuh de light! Ah thought he'd be too sick"—Sykes was muttering to himself when the whirr began again, closer, right underfoot this time. Long before this, Sykes' ability to think had been flattened down to primitive instinct and he leaped—onto the bed.

Outside Delia hears a cry that might have come from a maddened chimpanzee, a stricken gorilla. All the terror, all the horror, all the rage that man possibly could express, without a recognizable human sound.

A tremendous stir inside there, another series of animal screams, the intermittent whirr of the reptile. The shade torn violently down from the window, letting in the red dawn, a huge brown hand seizing the window stick, great dull blows upon the wooden floor punctuating the gibberish of sound long after the rattle of the snake had abruptly subsided. All this Delia could see and hear from her place beneath the window, and it made her ill. She crept over to the four-o'clocks and stretched herself on the cool earth to recover.

She lay there. "Delia, Delia!" She could hear Sykes calling in a most despairing tone as one who expected no answer. The sun crept on up, and he called. Delia could not move—her legs were gone flabby. She never moved, he called, and the sun kept rising.

"Mah Gawd!" she heard him moan. "Mah Gawd fum Heben!" She heard him stumbling about and got up from her flower-bed. The sun was growing warm. As she approached the door she heard him call out hopefully, "Delia, is dat you Ah heah?"

She saw him on his hands and knees as soon as she reached the door. He crept an inch or two toward her—all that he was able, and she saw his horribly swollen neck and his one open eye shining with hope. A surge of pity too strong to support bore her away from that eye that must, could not, fail to see the tubs. He would see the lamp. Orlando with its doctors was too far. She could scarcely reach the Chinaberry tree, where she waited in the growing heat while inside she knew the cold river was creeping up and up to extinguish that eye which must know by now that she knew.

[1926]

Taylor Plantan
Professor Diaz
English 170
1 April 2020

A Response to "Sweat"

Delia Jones, the protagonist of Zora Neale Hurston's "Sweat," seems to fear everything from the tiniest earthworm to her abusive husband, at least initially. However, her timid nature is quickly overshadowed by her resilience when she is faced with her husband's physical and psychological abuse. Though she appears apathetic, I think Delia actually feigns indifference, which gives her power in the story. Delia's occasional detachment from outward emotion allows her to continue to work to support the life she envisions for herself. In other words, rather than letting her rage consume and distract her from the physical, literal work that is at hand, she remains calm, giving herself the chance to also do the figurative work in battling the internal matrimonial and personal demons within herself and her husband.

Early on, Taylor focuses on what she's most interested in: namely, how Delia, who seems so submissive at first, is actually quite strong in her own way.

Delia's way of confronting life's complications is not only refreshing but also enlightening. Like most people, when I find myself in arguments, my intensity only grows as the conversation progresses. My energy and emotion build off of the other person, and I conversely feed his or her fervor; however, an understanding is eventually realized in order to move on with the day. Delia chooses another strategy: instead of exhausting her energy on anger, she chooses to continue with her work, nearly ignoring her husband completely.

Taylor considers her own experiences and how they differ from what she sees in the text.

The narrator uses omniscience in order to bring Delia's internal thoughts and conflicts to light. After a long day of battling with her husband and completing her work, Delia is retiring to bed when she recalls scenes from her marriage: the beating he gave her after just two months of marriage, the way Sykes has spent her hard-earned money, and his extramarital affair with Bertha. This invitation into Delia's psyche shapes how readers understand her motivations as a character. Through Delia's

Taylor uses specifics from the story to demonstrate her point.

recollections, we are able to see beyond the simple relaying of plot events and dialogue; we gain the history of Delia's marriage, Syke's character flaws, and the hardness that has slowly encased her over the years. By shifting away from the dialogue, the narrator is able to reveal Delia's mindset and the way in which she grapples with the day's events.

At this point, Delia's marriage is absent of love and consumed by Syke's lust for other women. The only thing that keeps her going is her religious faith in karma and "her little home" and the promise it holds for "her old days" (Hurston 56). Crawling into bed, Sykes wishes Delia goodnight the only way he knows how: by threatening her one last time for the day. Instead of provoking another fight, Delia simply turns over, satisfied by her "triumphant indifference to all that he was or did" (56).

Even in this informal response, Taylor cites textual evidence to support her ideas.

Delia is an expert in compartmentalizing all of her frustration, and it is quite remarkable to me. Feigning indifference to protect herself, Delia has a particular depth and resilience to her character. Her dedication to her work to secure a better future overpowers her matrimonial bond to her own husband. By the end of the story, she is more interested in retaining her status as the home owner and breadwinner than the traditional role of a subservient wife. Delia does not instinctively go out of her way to please her husband. By the end of the story, Delia is more interested in fully realizing the role of home owner than in continuing the traditional role of a subservient wife. The discovery of the snake in her house sends Delia fleeing in fright, but after she has time to reflect she is "quiet," and full of "coherent thought" that feeds a "cold, bloody rage" (62). When Sykes returns home, Delia, with her eye on the ultimate goal of independence, realizes what is going to happen to Sykes and allows it to happen, even momentarily looking him in the eye as he dies from the snake bite.

Taylor ends her response paper by landing on an interesting idea for a longer paper: Delia's commitment to financial independence overpowers her matrimonial bond.

Work Cited

Hurston, Zora Neale. "Sweat." *Reading and Writing about Literature: A Portable Guide*, edited by Janet E. Gardner and Joanne Diaz, 5th ed., Bedford/St. Martin's, 2021, pp. 54–63.

EXPLICATION

One common assignment is to perform an **explication** or a close reading of a poem or short prose passage. As the word implies, an *explication* takes what is implicit or subtle in a work of literature and makes it explicit and clear. Literary language tends to be densely packed with meaning, and your job as you explicate it is to unfold that meaning and lay it out for your reader. Explication allows you to "pop open the hood" of the poem, story, or play in order to observe how the machine works, and it is the key to understanding a complex literary work. The principal technique of explication is close reading; indeed, explication and close reading are so closely related that many writers use the words virtually interchangeably. When you write this sort of paper, you will examine a piece of literature, paying special attention to such elements of the language as sentence structure, *style*, *imagery*, *figurative language* (such as *similes* and *metaphors*), word choice, and perhaps even grammar and punctuation. The job of an explication is twofold: to point out particular, salient elements of style, and to explain the purpose and effect of these elements within the text.

When assigned an explication or a close reading, you might be tempted to simply walk through a text line by line, pointing out interesting features of style as they occur. A paper written in this way, though, can devolve into little more than summary or restatement of the literature in more prosaic language. A better idea is to isolate the various features of the literature on which you will focus and then deal separately with the specifics and implications of each.

The paper that follows is an example of a student essay that provides an explication of a literary text. First, take a look at Robert Herrick's "Upon Julia's Clothes," and then read the student's paper.

ROBERT HERRICK   [1591–1674]

Upon Julia's Clothes

When as in silks my Julia goes,
Then, then (methinks) how sweetly flows
That liquefaction of her clothes.

Next, when I cast mine eyes, and see
That brave vibration each way free,   5
O how that glittering taketh me!

[1648]

Jessica Barnes
Professor White
English 108
13 March 2020

Poetry in Motion: Herrick's "Upon Julia's Clothes"

In its brief six lines, Robert Herrick's "Upon Julia's Clothes" is a celebration of the physical sensuousness of the speaker's object of desire. The poem is structured like a seashell with two parts. In the first stanza, the speaker makes a seemingly simple observation: when Julia walks past, her silken clothes seem to flow as if they're liquid. In the second stanza, though, he provides a second observation: when Julia's body is "each way free" (2.5) of the clothing, the speaker is completely overtaken by the beauty of Julia's "brave vibration" (2.6).

Jessica's introduction lays out clearly the focus and structure of her paper.

Herrick provides several inversions of syntax to place emphasis on certain images. For example, in line 1, Herrick inverts "my Julia goes" with "in silks" to emphasize the importance of "silks" to Julia's sensuality. He creates another inversion in lines 2–3. The sense of the lines is as follows: "Then, then (methinks) that liquefaction of her clothes flows sweetly." Herrick rearranges the sentence to emphasize the sweetness of the flowing and to place the emphasis on "flows" and "clothes" at the ends of the lines.

In this paragraph, Jessica focuses on a specific language feature, syntax, and provides several examples from Herrick's poem.

Herrick also provides several changes in the iambic tetrameter meter to create varied lines within the poem's strict form. In line 2, he repeats "then" two times. In doing so, he forces the reader to pause deeply between each "then" and encourages the reader to meditate on the poet's decision to repeat the word in the first place. In line 6, too, Herrick alternately accelerates and decelerates the tempo of the line. The exclamatory "O" at the beginning of the line suggests that the speaker has been utterly charmed by Julia's beauty. It is a long sound that slows the reader down at the beginning of the line; in addition, it provides a stress on the first syllable of the line, instead of an unstressed syllable followed by a

This paragraph examines a different language feature, poetic meter.

Barnes 2

stressed one (see, for example, "That **brave** vibration" in line 5). "Glittering" also disrupts the strict tetrameter of the line. Its three syllables are compressed into two brief syllables ("**glitt**ering") so that the next accent can fall on "**tak**eth me," which emphasizes the fact that the speaker is totally overwhelmed by Julia's naked body.

Jessica begins to tie up her observations about specific language features with some preliminary analysis.

Ultimately, the poem reveals that Julia's beauty is beyond words. We cannot know whether Julia has actually taken her clothes off, or whether she has done so in the imagination of the speaker. Either way, the poem provides many sounds that mirror the "O" of line 6. The end rhyme for all of the lines in the first stanza rhyme with the "O": *goes, flows, clothes*. Each of these words reinforces the importance of Julia's shimmering beauty, and the power of her movements. The "ee" rhymes at the ends of the lines in stanza 2 — *see, free, me* — reinforce the idea that Julia's freedom in her nakedness also frees the poet's pleasure in imagining, or seeing, the "brave vibration" of her body.

The final language feature the paper examines is the repetition of vowel sounds.

Work Cited

Herrick, Robert. "Upon Julia's Clothes." *Reading and Writing about Literature: A Portable Guide*, edited by Janet E. Gardner and Joanne Diaz, 5th ed., Bedford/St. Martin's, 2021, p. 66.

ANALYSIS

To *analyze*, by definition, is to take something apart and examine how the individual parts relate to one another and function within the whole. Literary analysis allows you to closely read a text, focus in on one particular element, and create a thesis that argues for your analysis. As you read closely, start to isolate the key aspects of the text that interest you most — for example, **characterization**, **tone**, **dialogue**, or **imagery** — and begin to ask "How?" or "Why?" questions about that element. Then, gather evidence from the text in order to formulate an answer to your "How?" or "Why?" question.

Here, then, is how **explication** differs from **analysis**:

Explication	Analysis
Close reading of a literary text. This is where you "pop open the hood" of the poem, story, or play in order to observe how the machine works. This is your chance to tease out the layers of meaning in any given passage. Explication is the key to understanding a complex literary work and is the first step toward analysis.	A close reading of a literary text that focuses in on one element of the text and how it functions within the whole. A good analysis begins with a "how" or "why" question. You then attempt to answer this question with a thesis and evidence from the text.

Here is an example of a student essay that provides an analysis. First, take a look at Robert Browning's "My Last Duchess," then read the student's paper.

ROBERT BROWNING   [1812–1889]

My Last Duchess

Ferrara°

That's my last Duchess° painted on the wall,
Looking as if she were alive. I call
That piece a wonder, now: Frà Pandolf's° hands
Worked busily a day, and there she stands.
Will't please you sit and look at her? I said   5
"Frà Pandolf" by design, for never read

Ferrara: The poem is based on the events that occurred in the life of Alfonso II, duke of Ferrara in Italy, in the sixteenth century.
1. last Duchess: Ferrara's first wife, Lucrezia, died in 1561 at age seventeen after three years of marriage.
3. Frà Pandolf: Brother Pandolf, a fiction painter.

Strangers like you that pictured countenance,
The depth and passion of its earnest glance,
But to myself they turned (since none puts by
The curtain I have drawn for you, but I)   10
And seemed as they would ask me, if they durst,
How such a glance came there; so, not the first
Are you to turn and ask thus. Sir, 'twas not
Her husband's presence only, called that spot
Of joy into the Duchess' cheek: perhaps   15
Frà Pandolf chanced to say "Her mantle laps
Over my lady's wrist too much," or "Paint
Must never hope to reproduce the faint
Half-flush that dies along her throat": such stuff
Was courtesy, she thought, and cause enough   20
For calling up that spot of joy. She had
A heart—how shall I say?—too soon made glad,
Too easily impressed; she liked whate'er
She looked on, and her looks went everywhere.
Sir, 'twas all one! My favor at her breast,   25
The dropping of the daylight in the West,
The bough of cherries some officious fool
Broke in the orchard for her, the white mule
She rode with round the terrace—all and each
Would draw from her alike the approving speech,   30
Or blush, at least. She thanked men,—good! but thanked
Somehow—I know not how—as if she ranked
My gift of a nine-hundred-years-old name
With anybody's gift. Who'd stoop to blame
This sort of trifling? Even had you skill   35
In speech—(which I have not)—to make your will
Quite clear to such an one, and say, "Just this
Or that in you disgusts me; here you miss,
Or there exceed the mark"—and if she let
Herself be lessoned so, nor plainly set   40
Her wits to yours, forsooth, and made excuse,
—E'en then would be some stooping; and I choose
Never to stoop. Oh sir, she smiled, no doubt,
Whene'er I passed her; but who passed without
Much the same smile? This grew; I gave commands;   45
Then all smiles stopped together. There she stands

As if alive. Will't please you rise? We'll meet
The company below, then. I repeat,
The Count your master's known munificence
Is ample warrant that no just pretence   50
Of mine for dowry will be disallowed;
Though his fair daughter's self, as I avowed
At starting, is my object. Nay, we'll go
Together down, sir. Notice Neptune, though,
Taming a sea-horse, thought a rarity,   55
Which Claus of Innsbruck° cast in bronze for me!

[1842]

56. Claus of Innsbruck: A fictional sculptor.

Walker 1

Adam Walker
Professor Blitefield
English 203
22 February 2020

Possessed by the Need for Possession:
Browning's "My Last Duchess"

In "My Last Duchess," Robert Browning's duke reveals his
feelings of jealousy and betrayal as he discusses the duchess's portrait. In his dramatic monologue, the duke's public persona as an
aristocratic gentleman is shattered by the revelations of his actual
feelings about his dead duchess. The duke reveals what upsets him
most: his late wife's liberal smiles and attentions to others besides
himself. Though the duke offers a critique of his duchess's wantonness, the poem's use of dramatic irony reveals that it is his own jealousy and desire to control her that is the poem's central problem.

*The introduction
names the poem
to be analyzed
and clearly
explains that
the focus of the
paper will be the
duke's jealous
nature.*

Walker 2

The duke repeatedly calls attention to what he sees as the duchess's indiscretions. When the duke describes his wife's red cheeks in the portrait, he imagines the duchess as she sat for Fra Pandolf, and how she might have regarded his attention: "such stuff / Was courtesy, she thought, and cause enough / For calling up that spot of joy" (lines 19–21). According to the duke, the duchess mistook the painter's attentions as courtesies. Her blush, or "spot of joy" (21) on her cheeks, was too wanton for the duke. The duke admits that the duchess blushed at his own advances, but she also blushed at the painter, the "dropping of the daylight in the West" (26), a bough of cherries, and a white mule. The duchess's gaze is an indiscriminate one: she appreciates whatever pleases her, whether it be human, animal, or organic. This infuriates the duke, who thinks that his "nine-hundred-years-old name" (33) ought to make him more valuable in the eyes of the duchess.

Adam quotes specific lines from the poem in order to demonstrate his point. In each case, he integrates the quotation cleanly into his own prose.

The quotation is immediately followed by an explanation of its purpose in the paper.

Eventually, the duke feels the need to control the duchess's engagement with what attracts her, and he feels compelled to restrict the duchess's blushes with commands: "This grew; I gave commands; / Then all smiles stopped together. There she stands / As if alive" (45–47). These lines are concise and quick compared with the rhetoric of the other lines in the poem. Even so, they are in some ways the most important. What made the smiles stop? Was the duchess silenced in life? Or was it her death that stopped the smiling? And why does the duke need this portrait that resembles the duchess when she was alive?

Adam uses rhetorical questions to provide stylistic variety and to get the reader thinking.

Ultimately, the showing of the portrait is a way for the duke to show his possessions — and his command of his possessions — to the envoy of the Count. As the duke invites the envoy to come downstairs, he already characterizes his future bride as a kind of possession:

> I repeat,
> The Count your master's known munificence
> Is ample warrant that no just pretence
> Of mine for dowry will be disallowed;
> Though his fair daughter's self, as I avowed
> At starting, is my object. (48–53)

Note that the long quotation is blocked (indented from the left margin) and does not use quotation marks.

Walker 3

After alluding to the generous dowry that he will receive, the duke checks himself by saying that it is "his [the Count's] fair daughter's self" that he has found so compelling. Even so, the duke suggests that he will exert the same controls on her that he exerted on his late wife. Though the duke offers a critique of his duchess's wantonness, the poem's use of dramatic irony reveals that it is own jealousy and desire to control her that is the poem's central problem. In the end, she runs the same risk of becoming a sea horse that requires Neptune's taming.

Adam's concluding sentence alludes to the final lines of the poem.

Work Cited

Browning, Robert. "My Last Duchess." *Reading and Writing about Literature: A Portable Guide*, edited by Janet E. Gardner and Joanne Diaz, 5th ed., Bedford/St. Martin's, 2021, pp. 69–71.

COMPARISON AND CONTRAST

Another common paper assignment is the **comparison-and-contrast** essay. You might be asked to draw comparisons and contrasts within a single work of literature—say, between two characters in a story or play. Even more common is an assignment that asks you to compare and contrast a particular element—**characters**, **setting**, **style**, **tone**, and so on—in two or more stories, poems, or plays. A *comparison* emphasizes the similarities between two or more items, while a *contrast* highlights their differences. Though some papers do both, it is typical for an essay to emphasize one or the other.

If you are allowed to choose the works of literature for a comparison-and-contrast paper, take care to select works that have enough in common to make such a comparison interesting and valid. Even if Henrik Ibsen's *A Doll House* and Shirley Jackson's "The Lottery" are your favorites, it is difficult to imagine a well-focused paper comparing these two, as they share virtually nothing in terms of authorship, history, theme, or style, having been written in different genres, in different centuries, and on different continents. It would make far more sense to select two seventeenth-century poems or two love stories.

The paper that follows compares Robert Browning's "My Last Duchess" (pp. 69–71) and Christina Rossetti's "After Death." First, read Rossetti's poem; then read the following student paper:

CHRISTINA ROSSETTI   [1830–1894]

After Death

The curtains were half drawn, the floor was swept
   And strewn with rushes, rosemary and may°
Lay thick upon the bed on which I lay,
Where through the lattice ivy-shadows crept.
He leaned above me, thinking that I slept   5
   And could not hear him; but I heard him say,
   "Poor child, poor child": and as he turned away
Came a deep silence, and I knew he wept.
He did not touch the shroud, or raise the fold
   That hid my face, or take my hand in his,   10
     Or ruffle the smooth pillows for my head:
     He did not love me living; but once dead
He pitied me; and very sweet it is
To know he still is warm though I am cold.

[1849]

may: Green or flowering branches used for May Day celebrations.

Todd Bowen
Professor Harrison
English 215
12 May 2021

Speakers for the Dead: Narrators in
"My Last Duchess" and "After Death"

In "My Last Duchess," Robert Browning creates a duke whose tight control over his wife — and his preoccupation with his own noble rank — reveal a misogynistic character. Browning's dramatic monologue stands in stark contrast to Christina Rossetti's "After Death," a sonnet in which the speaker comes back from the dead to reveal what she observes about her lover. Using two very different modes of address in their poems, Browning and Rossetti suggest the restrictions placed on women in traditional marriages or male/female relationships in the Victorian patriarchal society.

Through the distinct perspectives of their poems, Browning and Rossetti create completely different portraits of women after death. In "My Last Duchess," the duke uses the actual portrait of his dead wife to describe a woman who smiled too liberally at men who fawned over her. The duke says, "She had / A heart — how shall I say? — too soon made glad, / Too easily impressed; she liked whate'er / She looked on, and her looks went everywhere" (lines 21–24). Throughout his long dramatic monologue, the duke meditates on several moments when the duchess betrays him by smiling at others; however, we as readers never get to hear the duchess's side of the story.

In Rossetti's "After Death," however, the tables are turned: the dead woman gets to speak back to the man who performs his grief over her death. In doing so, she carefully observes the behavior of her lover, who thinks that she is merely a lifeless corpse. In each line of the small sonnet, the speaker observes the man as he leans above her, says "Poor child, poor child" (line 7), and then turns away without actually touching her body. Even so, the woman suggests that this is an improvement from when she was alive: "He did not love me living; but once dead / He pitied me" (12–13). The speaker's final couplet is especially chilling: "and

Todd's concise introduction names the authors and poems that will be the subject of his comparison, as well as the paper's focus on certain shared features of the poems.

The first two body paragraphs each focus on one of the poems, providing a combination of specific evidence — mostly in the form of quotations — and analysis of this evidence.

Bowen 2

very sweet it is / To know he still is warm though I am cold" (13–14). *Note that Todd distinguishes between the poet Rossetti and the speaker of the poem.*

The speaker says that it is "sweet" to know that the man has outlived her. She doesn't explain this sweetness, but perhaps it is because she can observe his emotion in a way that she never could have while she was alive.

When read together, Rossetti's "After Death" and Browning's *The concluding paragraph contains the heart of the actual comparison of the poems.*

"My Last Duchess" function as companion pieces, each speaking to the other in a kind of call-and-response. Browning's duke shuts down any speech beyond his own, talking at length in the silence of the portrait and the visitor who looks at it. His story is the only story that he wants to present, even if his speech reveals his own shortcomings. Rossetti's woman provides an alternative perspective of death and mourning as the woman speaks from the dead to reveal the shortcomings of the man who mourns her. Through their distinct uses of voice and perspective, both poems provide critiques on the societal limits placed on women's agency in the Victorian period.

Works Cited

Browning, Robert. "My Last Duchess." *Reading and Writing about Literature: A Portable Guide*, edited by Janet E. Gardner and Joanne Diaz, 5th ed., Bedford/St. Martin's, 2021, pp. 69–71.

Rossetti, Christina. "After Death." Gardner and Diaz, p. 74.

ESSAY EXAMS

The key to getting through the potentially stressful situation of an essay exam is to be prepared and to know what will be expected of you.

Preparation takes two forms: knowing the material and anticipating the questions. Knowing the material starts with keeping up with all reading and homework assignments throughout the term. You can't possibly read several weeks' or months' worth of material the night before the test and hope to remember it all. The days before the test should be used not for catching up but for review—revisiting the readings, skimming or rereading key passages, and studying your class notes. It's best to break up study sessions into manageable blocks if possible. Reviewing for two hours a night for three nights before the exam will be far more effective than a single six-hour cram session on the eve of the test.

Anticipating the questions that might be on the exam is a bit trickier, but it can be done. What themes and issues have come up again and again in class lectures or discussions? What patterns do you see in your class notes? What points did your instructor stress? These are the topics most likely to appear on the exam. Despite what you might think, it is very rare that an instructor poses intentionally obscure exam questions in an attempt to trip up students or expose their ignorance. Most often, the instructor is providing you with an opportunity to demonstrate what you know, and you should be ready to take that opportunity.

Open-Book versus Closed-Book Exams

Your exam may be open-book or closed-book; find out in advance which it will be, so that you can plan and study accordingly. In an *open-book* exam, you are allowed to use your textbook during the exam. If you know the exam is going to be open-book, you might also jot down any important notes in the book itself, where you can find them readily if you need them. Use your textbook sparingly, though—just enough to find the evidence you know to be there. For a *closed-book* exam, you have to rely on your memory alone, but you should still try to be as specific as possible in your references to the literature, using character names, recalling plot elements, and so forth.

Develop a Plan

When you sit down to take the exam, you may have the urge to start writing right away, since your time is limited. Suppress that urge and read through the entire exam first, paying special attention to the instruction portion. Often the exam will offer you choices, such as "Answer two of the following three questions," or "Select a single poem as the basis of your answer." Once you are certain what is expected of you, take a few more minutes to plan your answers before you start writing. A few jotted notes or an informal outline may take a moment, but it will likely save you time as you write. If you are writing more than one essay, take care not to repeat yourself or to write more than one essay about any one piece of literature. The idea is to show your instructor your mastery of the course material, and to do so effectively, you should demonstrate an impressive breadth of knowledge.

Aim for Clarity

When you do begin writing, bear in mind that instructors have different expectations for exam answers than they do for essays written outside of class. They know that in timed exams you have no time for research or extensive revisions. Clarity and concision are the keys; an elegant prose style is not expected (though, of course, it will come as a pleasant surprise if you can manage it). Effective essay answers are often more formulaic than other sorts of effective writing, relying on the schematic of a straight-forward introduction, simple body paragraphs, and a brief conclusion.

Your introduction should be simple and to the point. A couple of sentences is generally all that is needed, and these should avoid rhetorical flourishes or digressions. Often the best strategy is to parrot back the instructions as an opening statement. Body paragraphs for essay answers should also be simple and will often, though not always, be briefer than they would be in an essay you worked on at home. They should still be as specific as possible, making reference to and perhaps even quoting the literature to illustrate your points. Just as in a more fully developed essay, try to avoid dwelling in generalities; use specific examples and evidence. Conclusions for essay exams are usually brief, often just a sentence or two of summary.

Watch the Time

Finally, take a watch with you on exam day and keep a close eye on the time. Use all the time you are given and budget it carefully. If you have an hour to write two answers, don't spend forty-five minutes on the first. Even though you will likely be pressed for time, save a few minutes at the end to proofread your answers. Make any corrections as neatly and legibly as possible. Watch the time, but try not to watch your classmates' progress. Keep focused on your own process. Just because someone else is using his or her book a lot, you shouldn't feel you need to do the same. If someone finishes early and leaves, don't take this as a sign that you are running behind or that you are less efficient or less smart than that person. Students who don't make full use of their exam time are often underprepared; they tend to write vague and underdeveloped answers and should not be your role models.

An open-book essay exam on poetry gave students several options, including "Select two poems by different poets, each of which deals with the theme of time, and compare how the authors present this theme." A student chose William Shakespeare's Sonnet 73 (p. 79) and Robert Herrick's "To the Virgins, to Make Much of Time" (pp. 79–80). Read the two poems and then the student's essay exam answer.

WILLIAM SHAKESPEARE   [1564–1616]

Sonnet 73

That time of year thou mayst in me behold
When yellow leaves, or none, or few, do hang
Upon those boughs which shake against the cold,
Bare ruined choirs,° where late° the sweet birds sang. *choir stalls/lately*
In me thou seest the twilight of such day   5
As after sunset fadeth in the west,
Which by and by black night doth take away,
Death's second self, that seals up all in rest.
In me thou seest the glowing of such fire
That on the ashes of his youth doth lie,   10
As the deathbed whereon it must expire,
Consumed with that which it was nourished by.
   This thou perceiv'st, which makes thy love more strong,
   To love that well which thou must leave ere long.

[1609]

ROBERT HERRICK   [1591–1674]

To the Virgins, to Make Much of Time

Gather ye rosebuds while ye may,
   Old time is still a-flying;
And this same flower that smiles today
   Tomorrow will be dying.
The glorious lamp of heaven, the sun,   5
   The higher he's a-getting,

The sooner will his race be run,
  And nearer he's to setting.
That age is best which is the first,
  When youth and blood are warmer;   10
But being spent, the worse, and worst
  Times still succeed the former.
Then be not coy, but use your time,
  And while ye may, go marry;
For having lost but once your prime,   15
  You may forever tarry.

[1648]

Midterm Essay: Option #2

Shakespeare's Sonnet 73 ("That time of year thou mayst in me behold") and Herrick's "To the Virgins, to Make Much of Time" both deal with the theme of time, and particularly the effect that time has on love. Though there are important differences in their focus and style, both poems urge their readers to love well and make the most of the time they have left.

Both poems make their points about time through a series of metaphors, and in fact they use some of the same metaphors from nature. Herrick begins with the image of rosebuds, which bloom and then die quickly. Shakespeare's first metaphor is also drawn from the world of plants, in this case a tree losing its leaves in the autumn. In the sonnet, the natural world is even connected to the spiritual world of church when the poet refers to the branches of the tree as "choirs" (line 4). Both poems also compare life to a single day, with the setting sun symbolizing death. Toward the end of his sonnet, Shakespeare writes of life as a fire that burns brightly in youth and then cools as a person nears death. While Herrick does not refer to fire specifically, he follows a similar line of reasoning when he mentions a time "When youth and blood are warmer" (3.10).

The introductory paragraph is brief and restates the assignment, adding in specifics to begin focusing the essay.

The two body paragraphs are also fairly brief, but they give lots of specific examples from the poems rather than relying on generalizations.

Because this was an open-book exam, the student was even able to incorporate brief quotations in her answer.

The most significant difference between the two poems lies in the characters of the speaker and the implied listener. Herrick offers his advice about the nature of time and its effect on love to "the Virgins" generally. He tells them to "go marry" (4.14) but he offers no specifics about whom they should be marrying or how they might choose these mates. Shakespeare's poem, on the other hand, seems to be addressed to a single "you" who is in some sort of relationship with the speaker, the "me" who narrates the poem. When he urges the listener "To love that well which thou must leave ere long" (14), he is referring to himself as the object of love.

The organization is clear and straightforward, with one body paragraph comparing similarities between the poems and one contrasting a key difference.

In the end, the differences end up overshadowing the superficial similarities of theme and purpose. Herrick's poem, with its relative lack of specificity, comes across as the sort of kindly advice an older person, perhaps an uncle, might give to any young man or woman. Shakespeare's is a more intimate, and ultimately somewhat darker, poem.

The conclusion is also simple in form and purpose; it restates the main points of the body paragraphs in new language and makes the contrast more explicit.

CHAPTER 5

Writing about Stories

Fiction has long been broken down and discussed in terms of specific elements common to all stories, and chances are you will be focusing on one or more of these when you write an essay about a story. (See Questions for Active Reading: Fiction, p. 8 for questions to consider when you write.)

ELEMENTS OF FICTION

The **elements of fiction** most commonly identified are **plot**, **character**, **point of view**, **setting**, **theme**, **symbolism**, and **style**. If you find yourself wondering what to write about a story, a good place to begin is isolating these elements and seeing how they work on a reader and how they combine to create the unique artifact that is a particular story.

Plot

While on some level we all read stories to find out what happens next, in truth, plot is usually the least interesting of the elements of fiction. Students who have little experience writing about fiction tend to spend too much time retelling the plot. You can avoid this by bearing in mind that your readers will also have read the literature in question and don't need a thorough replay of what happened. In general, readers just need small reminders of the key points of plot about which you will write, and these should serve as springboards into analysis and discussion. Still, writing about the plot sometimes makes sense, especially when the plot surprises your expectations by, for instance, rearranging the chronology of events or otherwise presenting things in nonrealistic ways. When this happens in a story, the plot may indeed prove fertile ground for analysis and may be the basis of an interesting paper.

Character

Many interesting essays analyze the actions, motivations, and development of individual characters. How does the author reveal a character to the reader? How does a character grow and develop over the course of a story? Readers have to carefully examine what insights the text provides about a character, but sometimes readers have to consider what's left out. What does the reader have to infer about the character that isn't explicitly written? What does the character refrain from saying? What secrets do characters keep from others, or from themselves? These questions can be fertile ground for analysis. Although the most obvious character to write about is usually the **protagonist**, don't let your imagination stop there. Often the **antagonist** or even a minor character can be an interesting object of study. Keep in mind, too, that characters can start out as antagonistic figures and experience a transformation in the eyes of the narrator or other characters, or in the eyes of the reader. Your job in writing a paper is to consider these transformations and try to understand why a text explores these complex character developments.

Point of View

Related to character is the issue of point of view. The perspective from which a story is told can make a big difference in how we perceive it. Sometimes a story is told in the *first person*, from the point of view of one of the characters. Whether this is a major character or a minor character, we must always remember that **first-person narrators** can be unreliable, as they do not have access to all vital information, and their own agendas can often skew the way they see events. A **third-person narrator** may be **omniscient**, knowing everything pertinent to a story; or limited, knowing, for instance, the thoughts and motives of the protagonist but not of any of the other characters. As you read a story, ask yourself what the point of view contributes and why the author may have chosen to present the story from a particular perspective.

Setting

Sometimes a setting is merely the backdrop for a story, but often place plays an important role in our understanding of a work. John Cheever chooses Midtown Manhattan in the mid-twentieth century as the setting of his story "Reunion." It is the perfect milieu for an exploration of urban space and its effects on the relationship between the father and son in that story, and the plot very likely would have taken a very different turn if the story had been set, say, in the Pacific Northwest. As you read, ask yourself how significant a setting is and what it adds to the meaning of a story. Remember that setting refers to time as well as place.

Theme

All **short stories** have at least one theme—an abstract concept such as *love*, *war*, *friendship*, *revenge*, or *art*—brought to life and made real through the plot, characters, and so on. Identifying a theme or themes is one of the first keys to understanding a story, but it is not the end point. Pay some attention to how the theme is developed. Is it blatant or subtle? What actions, events, or symbols make the theme apparent to you? Generally, the driving force of a story is the author's desire to convey something *about* a particular theme, to make readers think and feel in a certain way. First ask yourself what the author seems to be saying about love or war or whatever themes you have noted; second, whether you agree with the author's perceptions; and finally, why or why not.

Symbolism

Some students get frustrated when their instructors or their class-mates begin to talk about **symbolism**. How do we know that an author intended a symbolic reading? Maybe that flower is just a real flower, not a stand-in for youth or for life and regeneration as some readers insist. And even if it is a symbol, how do we know we are reading it correctly? While it's true that plenty of flowers *are* simply flowers, and while students should identify symbols with caution, the more prom-inent an image in a story, the more likely it is meant to be read sym-bolically. Careful writers choose their words and images for maximum impact, filling them with as much meaning as possible and inviting their readers to interpret them. When John Steinbeck entitles his story "The Chrysanthemums," we would do well to ask if the flow-ers are really just plants or if we are being asked to look for a greater significance.

Style

The final element of fiction isolated here is style, sometimes spoken of under the heading of tone or language. A text may strike you as sad or lighthearted, formal or casual. It may make you feel nostalgic, or it may make your heart race with excitement. Somewhat more difficult, though, is isolating the elements of language that contribute to a partic-ular tone or effect. Look for characteristic stylistic elements that create these effects. Is the diction elevated and difficult, or ordinary and sim-ple? Are the sentences long and complex, or short and to the point? Is there dialogue? If so, how do the characters who speak this dialogue come across? Does the style stay consistent throughout the story, or does it change? What does the author leave out? Paying close attention to linguistic matters like these will take you far in your understanding of how a particular story achieves its effect.

STORIES FOR ANALYSIS

Read Charlotte Perkins Gilman's "The Yellow Wallpaper"(below) and Kate Chopin's "The Story of an Hour" (pp. 99–101), which we have annotated below. Both stories explore issues of women's identities and freedom. The questions following the annotated story ask you to analyze how the elements of fiction work in these two stories.

CHARLOTTE PERKINS GILMAN   [1860–1935]

The Yellow Wallpaper

It is very seldom that mere ordinary people like John and myself secure ancestral halls for the summer.

A colonial mansion, a hereditary estate, I would say a haunted house and reach the height of romantic felicity—but that would be asking too much of fate!

Still I will proudly declare that there is something queer about it.

Else, why should it be let so cheaply? And why have stood so long untenanted?

John laughs at me, of course, but one expects that in marriage.

John is practical in the extreme. He has no patience with faith, an intense horror of superstition, and he scoffs openly at any talk of things not to be felt and seen and put down in figures.

John is a physician, and *perhaps*—(I would not say it to a living soul, of course, but this is dead paper and a great relief to my mind)—*perhaps* that is one reason I do not get well faster.

You see, he does not believe I am sick!

And what can one do?

If a physician of high standing, and one's own husband, assures friends and relatives that there is really nothing the matter with one but temporary nervous depression—a slight hysterical tendency—what is one to do?

My brother is also a physician, and also of high standing, and he says the same thing.

So I take phosphates or phosphites—whichever it is, and tonics, and journeys, and air, and exercise, and am absolutely forbidden to "work" until I am well again.

Personally, I disagree with their ideas.

Personally, I believe that congenial work, with excitement and change, would do me good.

But what is one to do?

I did write for a while in spite of them; but it *does* exhaust me a good deal—having to be so sly about it, or else meet with heavy opposition.

I sometimes fancy that in my condition if I had less opposition and more society and stimulus—but John says the very worst thing I can do is to think about my condition, and I confess it always makes me feel bad.

So I will let it alone and talk about the house.

The most beautiful place! It is quite alone, standing well back from the road, quite three miles from the village. It makes me think of English places that you read about, for there are hedges and walls and gates that lock, and lots of separate little houses for the gardeners and people.

There is a *delicious* garden! I never saw such a garden—large and shady, full of box-bordered paths, and lined with long grape-covered arbors with seats under them.

There were greenhouses, too, but they are all broken now.

There was some legal trouble, I believe, something about the heirs and co-heirs; anyhow, the place has been empty for years.

That spoils my ghostliness, I am afraid, but I don't care—there is something strange about the house—I can feel it.

I even said so to John one moonlight evening, but he said what I felt was a *draught*, and shut the window.

I get unreasonably angry with John sometimes. I'm sure I never used to be so sensitive. I think it is due to this nervous condition.

But John says if I feel so, I shall neglect proper self-control; so I take pains to control myself—before him, at least, and that makes me very tired.

I don't like our room a bit. I wanted one downstairs that opened on the piazza and had roses all over the window, and such pretty old-fashioned chintz hangings! but John would not hear of it.

He said there was only one window and not room for two beds, and no near room for him if he took another.

He is very careful and loving, and hardly lets me stir without special direction.

I have a schedule prescription for each hour in the day; he takes all care from me, and so I feel basely ungrateful not to value it more.

He said we came here solely on my account, that I was to have perfect rest and all the air I could get. "Your exercise depends on your strength, my dear," said he, "and your food somewhat on your appetite; but air you can absorb all the time." So we took the nursery at the top of the house.

It is a big, airy room, the whole floor nearly, with windows that look all ways, and air and sunshine galore. It was nursery first and then playroom and gymnasium, I should judge; for the windows are barred for little children, and there are rings and things in the walls.

The paint and paper look as if a boys' school had used it. It is stripped off—the paper—in great patches all around the head of my bed, about as far as I can reach, and in a great place on the other side of the room low down. I never saw a worse paper in my life.

One of those sprawling flamboyant patterns committing every artistic sin.

It is dull enough to confuse the eye in following, pronounced enough to constantly irritate and provoke study, and when you follow the lame uncertain curves for a little distance they suddenly commit suicide—plunge off at outrageous angles, destroy themselves in unheard of contradictions.

The color is repellant, almost revolting; a smouldering unclean yellow, strangely faded by the slow-turning sunlight.

It is a dull yet lurid orange in some places, a sickly sulphur tint in others.

No wonder the children hated it! I should hate it myself if I had to live in this room long.

There comes John, and I must put this away,—he hates to have me write a word.

We have been here two weeks, and I haven't felt like writing before, since that first day.

I am sitting by the window now, up in this atrocious nursery, and there is nothing to hinder my writing as much as I please, save lack of strength.

John is away all day, and even some nights when his cases are serious.

I am glad my case is not serious!

But these nervous troubles are dreadfully depressing.

John does not know how much I really suffer. He knows there is no *reason* to suffer, and that satisfies him.

Of course it is only nervousness. It does weigh on me so not to do my duty in any way!

I meant to be such a help to John, such a real rest and comfort, and here I am a comparative burden already!

Nobody would believe what an effort it is to do what little I am able,—to dress and entertain, and order things.

It is fortunate Mary is so good with the baby. Such a dear baby!

And yet I *cannot* be with him, it makes me so nervous.

I suppose John never was nervous in his life. He laughs at me so about this wallpaper!

At first he meant to repaper the room, but afterward he said that I was letting it get the better of me, and that nothing was worse for a nervous patient than to give way to such fancies.

He said that after the wallpaper was changed it would be the heavy bedstead, and then the barred windows, and then that gate at the head of the stairs, and so on.

"You know the place is doing you good," he said, "and really, dear, I don't care to renovate the house just for a three months' rental."

"Then do let us go downstairs," I said, "there are such pretty rooms there."

Then he took me in his arms and called me a blessed little goose, and said he would go down cellar, if I wished, and have it white-washed into the bargain.

But he is right enough about the beds and windows and things.

It is an airy and comfortable room as anyone need wish, and, of course, I would not be so silly as to make him uncomfortable just for a whim.

I'm really getting quite fond of the big room, all but that horrid paper.

Out of one window I can see the garden, those mysterious deep-shaded arbors, the riotous old-fashioned flowers, and bushes and gnarly trees.

Out of another I get a lovely view of the bay and a little private wharf belonging to the estate. There is a beautiful shaded lane that runs down there from the house. I always fancy I see people walking in these numerous paths and arbors, but John has cautioned me not to give way to fancy in the least. He says that with my imaginative power and habit of story-making, a nervous weakness like mine is sure to lead to all manner of excited fancies, and that I ought to use my will and good sense to check the tendency. So I try.

I think sometimes that if I were only well enough to write a little it would relieve the press of ideas and rest me.

But I find I get pretty tired when I try.

It is so discouraging not to have any advice and companionship about my work. When I get really well, John says we will ask Cousin Henry and

Julia down for a long visit; but he says he would as soon put fireworks in my pillow-case as to let me have those stimulating people about now.

I wish I could get well faster.

But I must not think about that. This paper looks to me as if it *knew* what a vicious influence it had!

There is a recurrent spot where the pattern lolls like a broken neck and two bulbous eyes stare at you upside down.

I get positively angry with the impertinence of it and the everlasting-ness. Up and down and sideways they crawl, and those absurd, unblink-ing eyes are everywhere. There is one place where two breadths didn't match, and the eyes go all up and down the line, one a little higher than the other.

I never saw so much expression in an inanimate thing before, and we all know how much expression they have! I used to lie awake as a child and get more entertainment and terror out of blank walls and plain fur-niture than most children could find in a toy-store.

I remember what a kindly wink the knobs of our big, old bureau used to have, and there was one chair that always seemed like a strong friend.

I used to feel that if any of the other things looked too fierce I could always hop into that chair and be safe.

The furniture in this room is no worse than inharmonious, however, for we had to bring it all from downstairs. I suppose when this was used as a playroom they had to take the nursery things out, and no wonder! I never saw such ravages as the children have made here.

The wallpaper, as I said before, is torn off in spots, and it sticketh closer than a brother—they must have had perseverance as well as hatred.

Then the floor is scratched and gouged and splintered, the plaster itself is dug out here and there, and this great heavy bed, which is all we found in the room, looks as if it had been through the wars.

But I don't mind it a bit—only the paper.

There comes John's sister. Such a dear girl as she is, and so careful of me! I must not let her find me writing.

She is a perfect and enthusiastic housekeeper, and hopes for no better profession. I verily believe she thinks it is the writing which made me sick!

But I can write when she is out, and see her a long way off from these windows.

There is one that commands the road, a lovely shaded winding road, and one that just looks off over the country. A lovely country, too, full of great elms and velvet meadows.

This wallpaper has a kind of sub-pattern in a different shade, a par-ticularly irritating one, for you can only see it in certain lights, and not clearly then.

But in the places where it isn't faded and where the sun is just so—I can see a strange, provoking, formless sort of figure, that seems to skulk about behind that silly and conspicuous front design.

There's sister on the stairs!

Well, the Fourth of July is over! The people are all gone and I am tired out. John thought it might do me good to see a little company, so we just had mother and Nellie and the children down for a week.

Of course I didn't do a thing. Jennie sees to everything now.

But it tired me all the same.

John says if I don't pick up faster he shall send me to Weir Mitchell° in the fall.

But I don't want to go there at all. I had a friend who was in his hands once, and she says he is just like John and my brother, only more so!

Besides, it is such an undertaking to go so far.

I don't feel as if it was worthwhile to turn my hand over for anything, and I'm getting dreadfully fretful and querulous.

I cry at nothing, and cry most of the time.

Of course I don't when John is here, or anybody else, but when I am alone.

And I am alone a good deal just now. John is kept in town very often by serious cases, and Jennie is good and lets me alone when I want her to.

So I walk a little in the garden or down that lovely lane, sit on the porch under the roses, and lie down up here a good deal.

I'm getting really fond of the room in spite of the wallpaper. Perhaps *because* of the wallpaper.

It dwells in my mind so!

I lie here on this great immovable bed—it is nailed down, I believe—and follow that pattern about by the hour. It is as good as gymnastics, I assure you. I start, we'll say, at the bottom, down in the corner over there where it has not been touched, and I determine for the thousandth time that I *will* follow that pointless pattern to some sort of a conclusion.

I know a little of the principle of design, and I know this thing was not arranged on any laws of radiation, or alternation, or repetition, or symmetry, or anything else that I ever heard of.

It is repeated, of course, by the breadths, but not otherwise.

Looked at in one way each breadth stands alone, the bloated curves and flourishes—a kind of "debased Romanesque" with *delirium tremens*—go waddling up and down in isolated columns of fatuity.

Weir Mitchell: Dr. S. Weir Mitchell (1829–1914) was an American neurologist and author who advocated "rest cures" for nervous illnesses.

But, on the other hand, they connect diagonally, and the sprawling outlines run off in great slanting waves of optic horror, like a lot of wallowing sea-weeds in full chase.

The whole thing goes horizontally, too, at least it seems so, and I exhaust myself in trying to distinguish the order of its going in that direction.

They have used a horizontal breadth for a frieze, and that adds wonderfully to the confusion.

There is one end of the room where it is almost intact, and there, when the crosslights fade and the low sun shines directly upon it, I can almost fancy radiation after all,—the interminable grotesques seem to form around a common centre and rush off in headlong plunges of equal distraction.

It makes me tired to follow it. I will take a nap I guess.

I don't know why I should write this.

I don't want to.

I don't feel able.

And I know John would think it absurd. But I *must* say what I feel and think in some way—it is such a relief!

But the effort is getting to be greater than the relief.

Half the time now I am awfully lazy, and lie down ever so much.

John says I mustn't lose my strength, and has me take cod liver oil and lots of tonics and things, to say nothing of ale and wine and rare meat.

Dear John! He loves me very dearly, and hates to have me sick. I tried to have a real earnest reasonable talk with him the other day, and tell him how I wish he would let me go and make a visit to Cousin Henry and Julia.

But he said I wasn't able to go, nor able to stand it after I got there; and I did not make out a very good case for myself, for I was crying before I had finished.

It is getting to be a great effort for me to think straight. Just this nervous weakness I suppose.

And dear John gathered me up in his arms, and just carried me upstairs and laid me on the bed, and sat by me and read to me till it tired my head.

He said I was his darling and his comfort and all he had, and that I must take care of myself for his sake, and keep well.

He says no one but myself can help me out of it, that I must use my will and self-control and not let any silly fancies run away with me.

There's one comfort, the baby is well and happy, and does not have to occupy this nursery with the horrid wallpaper.

If we had not used it, that blessed child would have! What a fortunate escape! Why, I wouldn't have a child of mine, an impressionable little thing, live in such a room for worlds.

I never thought of it before, but it is lucky that John kept me here after all, I can stand it so much easier than a baby, you see.

Of course I never mention it to them any more — I am too wise, but I keep watch of it all the same.

There are things in the wallpaper that nobody knows but me, or ever will.

Behind that outside pattern the dim shapes get clearer every day.

It is always the same shape, only very numerous.

And it is like a woman stooping down and creeping about behind that pattern. I don't like it a bit. I wonder — I begin to think — I wish John would take me away from here!

It is so hard to talk with John about my case, because he is so wise, and because he loves me so.

But I tried it last night.

It was moonlight. The moon shines in all around just as the sun does.

I hate to see it sometimes, it creeps so slowly, and always comes in by one window or another.

John was asleep and I hated to waken him, so I kept still and watched the moonlight on that undulating wallpaper till I felt creepy.

The faint figure behind seemed to shake the pattern, just as if she wanted to get out.

I got up softly and went to feel and see if the paper *did* move, and when I came back John was awake.

"What is it, little girl?" he said. "Don't go walking about like that — you'll get cold."

I thought it was a good time to talk, so I told him that I really was not gaining here, and that I wished he would take me away.

"Why, darling!" said he, "our lease will be up in three weeks, and I can't see how to leave before.

"The repairs are not done at home, and I cannot possibly leave town just now. Of course if you were in any danger, I could and would, but you really are better, dear, whether you can see it or not. I am a doctor, dear, and I know. You are gaining flesh and color, your appetite is better, I feel really much easier about you."

"I don't weigh a bit more," said I, "nor as much; and my appetite may be better in the evening when you are here but it is worse in the morning when you are away!"

"Bless her little heart!" said he with a big hug, "she shall be as sick as she pleases! But now let's improve the shining hours by going to sleep, and talk about it in the morning!"

"And you won't go away?" I asked gloomily.

"Why, how can I, dear? It is only three weeks more and then we will take a nice little trip of a few days while Jennie is getting the house ready. Really dear you are better!"

"Better in body perhaps—" I began, and stopped short, for he sat up straight and looked at me with such a stern, reproachful look that I could not say another word.

"My darling," said he, "I beg you, for my sake and for our child's sake, as well as for your own, that you will never for one instant let that idea enter your mind! There is nothing so dangerous, so fascinating, to a temperament like yours. It is a false and foolish fancy. Can you trust me as a physician when I tell you so?"

So of course I said no more on that score, and we went to sleep before long. He thought I was asleep first, but I wasn't, and lay there for hours trying to decide whether that front pattern and the back pattern really did move together or separately.

On a pattern like this, by daylight, there is a lack of sequence, a defiance of law, that is a constant irritant to a normal mind.

The color is hideous enough, and unreliable enough, and infuriating enough, but the pattern is torturing.

You think you have mastered it, but just as you get well underway in following, it turns a back-somersault and there you are. It slaps you in the face, knocks you down, and tramples upon you. It is like a bad dream.

The outside pattern is a florid arabesque, reminding one of a fungus. If you can imagine a toadstool in joints, an interminable string of toadstools, budding and sprouting in endless convolutions—why, that is something like it.

That is, sometimes!

There is one marked peculiarity about this paper, a thing nobody seems to notice but myself, and that is that it changes as the light changes.

When the sun shoots in through the east window—I always watch for that first long, straight ray—it changes so quickly that I never can quite believe it.

That is why I watch it always.

By moonlight—the moon shines in all night when there is a moon—I wouldn't know it was the same paper.

At night in any kind of light, in twilight, candlelight, lamplight, and worst of all by moonlight, it becomes bars! The outside pattern I mean, and the woman behind it is as plain as can be.

I didn't realize for a long time what the thing was that showed behind, that dim sub-pattern, but now I am quite sure it is a woman.

By daylight she is subdued, quiet. I fancy it is the pattern that keeps her so still. It is so puzzling. It keeps me quiet by the hour.

I lie down ever so much now. John says it is good for me, and to sleep all I can.

Indeed he started the habit by making me lie down for an hour after each meal.

It is a very bad habit I am convinced, for you see I don't sleep.

And that cultivates deceit, for I don't tell them I'm awake—O, no!

The fact is I am getting a little afraid of John.

He seems very queer sometimes, and even Jennie has an inexplicable look.

It strikes me occasionally, just as a scientific hypothesis,—that perhaps it is the paper!

I have watched John when he did not know I was looking, and come into the room suddenly on the most innocent excuses, and I've caught him several times *looking at the paper*! And Jennie too. I caught Jennie with her hand on it once.

She didn't know I was in the room, and when I asked her in a quiet, a very quiet voice, with the most restrained manner possible, what she was doing with the paper—she turned around as if she had been caught stealing, and looked quite angry—asked me why I should frighten her so!

Then she said that the paper stained everything it touched, that she had found yellow smooches on all my clothes and John's, and she wished we would be more careful!

Did not that sound innocent? But I know she was studying that pattern, and I am determined that nobody shall find it out but myself!

Life is very much more exciting now than it used to be. You see I have something more to expect, to look forward to, to watch. I really do eat better, and am more quiet than I was.

John is so pleased to see me improve! He laughed a little the other day, and said I seemed to be flourishing in spite of my wallpaper.

I turned it off with a laugh. I had no intention of telling him it was *because* of the wallpaper—he would make fun of me. He might even want to take me away.

I don't want to leave now until I have found it out. There is a week more, and I think that will be enough.

I'm feeling ever so much better! I don't sleep much at night, for it is so interesting to watch developments; but I sleep a good deal in the daytime.

In the daytime it is tiresome and perplexing.

There are always new shoots on the fungus, and new shades of yellow all over it. I cannot keep count of them, though I have tried conscientiously.

It is the strangest yellow, that wallpaper! It makes me think of all the yellow things I ever saw — not beautiful ones like buttercups, but old foul, bad yellow things.

But there is something else about that paper — the smell! I noticed it the moment we came into the room, but with so much air and sun it was not bad. Now we have had a week of fog and rain, and whether the windows are open or not, the smell is here.

It creeps all over the house.

I find it hovering in the dining-room, skulking in the parlor, hiding in the hall, lying in wait for me on the stairs.

It gets into my hair.

Even when I go to ride, if I turn my head suddenly and surprise it — there is that smell!

Such a peculiar odor, too! I have spent hours in trying to analyze it, to find what it smelled like.

It is not bad — at first, and very gentle, but quite the subtlest, most enduring odor I ever met.

In this damp weather it is awful, I wake up in the night and find it hanging over me.

It used to disturb me at first. I thought seriously of burning the house — to reach the smell.

But now I am used to it. The only thing I can think of that it is like is the *color* of the paper! A yellow smell.

There is a very funny mark on this wall, low down, near the mop-board. A streak that runs round the room. It goes behind every piece of furniture, except the bed, a long, straight, even *smooch*, as if it had been rubbed over and over.

I wonder how it was done and who did it, and what they did it for. Round and round and round — round and round and round — it makes me dizzy!

I really have discovered something at last.

Through watching so much at night, when it changes so, I have finally found out.

The front pattern *does* move — and no wonder! The woman behind shakes it!

Sometimes I think there are a great many women behind, and sometimes only one, and she crawls around fast, and her crawling shakes it all over.

Then in the very bright spots she keeps still, and in the very shady spots she just takes hold of the bars and shakes them hard.

And she is all the time trying to climb through. But nobody could climb through that pattern—it strangles so; I think that is why it has so many heads.

They get through, and then the pattern strangles them off and turns them upside down, and makes their eyes white!

If those heads were covered or taken off it would not be half so bad.

I think that woman gets out in the daytime!

And I'll tell you why—privately—I've seen her!

I can see her out of every one of my windows!

It is the same woman, I know, for she is always creeping, and most women do not creep by daylight.

I see her in that long shaded lane, creeping up and down. I see her in those dark grape arbors, creeping all around the garden.

I see her on that long road under the trees, creeping along, and when a carriage comes she hides under the blackberry vines.

I don't blame her a bit. It must be very humiliating to be caught creeping by daylight!

I always lock the door when I creep by daylight. I can't do it at night, for I know John would suspect something at once.

And John is so queer now, that I don't want to irritate him. I wish he would take another room! Besides, I don't want anybody to get that woman out at night but myself.

I often wonder if I could see her out of all the windows at once.

But, turn as fast as I can, I can only see out of one at one time.

And though I always see her, she *may* be able to creep faster than I can turn!

I have watched her sometimes away off in the open country, creeping as fast as a cloud shadow in a high wind.

If only that top pattern could be gotten off from the under one! I mean to try it, little by little.

I have found out another funny thing, but I shan't tell it this time! It does not do to trust people too much.

There are only two more days to get this paper off, and I believe John is beginning to notice. I don't like the look in his eyes.

And I heard him ask Jennie a lot of professional questions, about me. She had a very good report to give.

She said I slept a good deal in the daytime.

John knows I don't sleep very well at night, for all I'm so quiet!

He asked me all sorts of questions too, and pretended to be very loving and kind.

As if I couldn't see through him!

Still, I don't wonder he acts so, sleeping under this paper for three months.

It only interests me, but I feel sure John and Jennie are secretly affected by it.

Hurrah! This is the last day, but it is enough. John is to stay in town over night, and won't be out until this evening.

Jennie wanted to sleep with me—the sly thing! But I told her I should undoubtedly rest better for a night all alone.

That was clever, for really I wasn't alone a bit! As soon as it was moonlight and that poor thing began to crawl and shake the pattern, I got up and ran to help her.

I pulled and she shook, I shook and she pulled, and before morning we had peeled off yards of that paper.

A strip about as high as my head and half around the room.

And then when the sun came and that awful pattern began to laugh at me, I declared I would finish it to-day!

We go away to-morrow, and they are moving all my furniture down again to leave things as they were before.

Jennie looked at the wall in amazement, but I told her merrily that I did it out of pure spite at the vicious thing.

She laughed and said she wouldn't mind doing it herself, but I must not get tired.

How she betrayed herself that time!

But I am here, and no person touches this paper but me,—not *alive*!

She tried to get me out of the room—it was too patent! But I said it was so quiet and empty and clean now that I believed I would lie down again and sleep all I could, and not to wake me even for dinner—I would call when I woke.

So now she is gone, and the servants are gone, and the things are gone, and there is nothing left but that great bedstead nailed down, with the canvas mattress we found on it.

We shall sleep downstairs to-night, and take the boat home to-morrow.

I quite enjoy the room, now it is bare again.

How those children did tear about here!

This bedstead is fairly gnawed!

But I must get to work.

I have locked the door and thrown the key down into the front path.

I don't want to go out, and I don't want to have anybody come in, till John comes.

I want to astonish him.

I've got a rope up here that even Jennie did not find. If that woman does get out, and tries to get away, I can tie her!

But I forgot I could not reach far without anything to stand on!

This bed will *not* move!

I tried to lift and push it until I was lame, and then I got so angry I bit off a little piece at one corner—but it hurt my teeth.

Then I peeled off all the paper I could reach standing on the floor. It sticks horribly and the pattern just enjoys it! All those strangled heads and bulbous eyes and waddling fungus growths just shriek with derision!

I am getting angry enough to do something desperate. To jump out of the window would be admirable exercise, but the bars are too strong even to try.

Besides I wouldn't do it. Of course not. I know well enough that a step like that is improper and might be misconstrued.

I don't like to *look* out of the windows even—there are so many of those creeping women, and they creep so fast.

I wonder if they all come out of that wallpaper as I did?

But I am securely fastened now by my well-hidden rope—you don't get *me* out in the road there!

I suppose I shall have to get back behind the pattern when it comes night, and that is hard!

It is so pleasant to be out in this great room and creep around as I please!

I don't want to go outside. I won't, even if Jennie asks me to.

For outside you have to creep on the ground, and everything is green instead of yellow.

But here I can creep smoothly on the floor, and my shoulder just fits in that long smooch around the wall, so I cannot lose my way.

Why, there's John at the door!

It is no use, young man, you can't open it!

How he does call and pound!

Now he's crying for an axe.

It would be a shame to break down that beautiful door!

"John dear!" said I in the gentlest voice, "the key is down by the front steps, under a plantain leaf!"

That silenced him for a few moments.

Then he said—very quietly indeed, "Open the door, my darling!"

"I can't," said I. "The key is down by the front door under a plantain leaf!"

And then I said it again, several times, very gently and slowly, and said it so often that he had to go and see, and he got it of course, and came in. He stopped short by the door.

"What is the matter?" he cried. "For God's sake, what are you doing!"

I kept on creeping just the same, but I looked at him over my shoulder.

"I've got out at last," said I, "in spite of you and Jane. And I've pulled off most of the paper, so you can't put me back!"

Now why should that man have fainted? But he did, and right across my path by the wall, so that I had to creep over him every time!

[1892]

KATE CHOPIN   [1851–1904]

The Story of an Hour

Knowing that Mrs. Mallard was afflicted with a heart trouble, great care was taken to break to her as gently as possible the news of her husband's death.

It was her sister Josephine who told her, in broken sentences; veiled hints that revealed in half concealing. Her husband's friend Richards was there, too, near her. It was he who had been in the newspaper office when intelligence of the railroad disaster was received, with Brently Mallard's name leading the list of "killed." He had only taken the time to assure himself of its truth by a second telegram, and had hastened to forestall any less careful, less tender friend in bearing the sad message.

Her family and friends seem to think she's delicate.

She did not hear the story as many women have heard the same, with a paralyzed inability to accept its significance. She wept at once, with sudden, wild abandonment, in her sister's arms. When the storm of grief had spent itself she went away to her room alone. She would have no one follow her.

There stood, facing the open window, a comfortable, roomy armchair. Into this she sank, pressed down by a physical exhaustion that haunted her body and seemed to reach into her soul.

She could see in the open square before her house the tops of trees that were all aquiver with the new spring life. The delicious breath of rain was in the air. In the street below a peddler was crying his wares. The notes of a distant song which some one was singing reached her faintly, and countless sparrows were twittering in the eaves.

A beautiful day. Why does Chopin take the time to describe it in such a short story, especially one about a death?

There were patches of blue sky showing here and there through the clouds that had met and piled one above the other in the west facing her window.

She sat with her head thrown back upon the cushion of the chair, quite motionless, except when a sob came up into her throat and shook her, as a child who had cried itself to sleep continues to sob in its dreams.

She was young, with a fair, calm face, whose lines bespoke repression and even a certain strength. But now there was a dull stare in her eyes, whose gaze was fixed away off yonder on one of those patches of blue sky. It was not a glance of reflection, but rather indicated a suspension of intelligent thought.

There was something coming to her and she was waiting for it, fearfully. What was it? She did not know; it was too subtle and elusive to name. But she felt it, creeping out of the sky, reaching toward her through the sounds, the scents, the color that filled the air.

Ominous. What could be coming? Something physical or emotional?

Now her bosom rose and fell tumultuously. She was beginning to recognize this thing that was approaching to possess her, and she was striving to beat it back with her will—as powerless as her two white slender hands would have been.

When she abandoned herself a little whispered word escaped her slightly parted lips. She said it over and over under her breath: "free, free, free!" The vacant stare and the look of terror that had followed it went from her eyes. They stayed keen and bright. Her pulses beat fast, and the coursing blood warmed and relaxed every inch of her body.

She did not stop to ask if it were or were not a monstrous joy that held her. A clear and exalted perception enabled her to dismiss the suggestion as trivial.

How could it be joy? Her emotions seem quick to change and hard to keep up with, even for her.

She knew that she would weep again when she saw the kind, tender hands folded in death; the face that had never looked save with love upon her, fixed and gray and dead. But she saw beyond that bitter moment a long procession of years to come that would belong to her absolutely. And she opened and spread her arms out to them in welcome.

There would be no one to live for her during those coming years: she would live for herself. There would be no powerful will bending hers in that blind persistence with which men and women believe they have a right to impose a private will upon a fellow-creature. A kind intention or a cruel intention made the act seem no less a crime as she looked upon it in that brief moment of illumination.

And yet she had loved him—sometimes. Often she had not. What did it matter! What could love, the unsolved mystery, count for in face of this possession of self-assertion which she suddenly recognized as the strongest impulse of her being!

"Free! Body and soul free!" she kept whispering.

Josephine was kneeling before the closed door with her lips to the keyhole, imploring for admission. "Louise, open the door! I beg; open the door—you will make yourself ill. What are you doing, Louise? For heaven's sake open the door."

"Go away. I am not making myself ill." No; she was drinking in a very elixir of life through that open window.

Her fancy was running riot along those days ahead of her. Spring days, and summer days, and all sorts of days that would be her own. She breathed a quick prayer that life might be long. It was only yesterday she had thought with a shudder that life might be long.

She arose at length and opened the door to her sister's importunities. There was a feverish triumph in her eyes, and she carried herself unwittingly like a goddess of Victory. She clasped her sister's waist, and together they descended the stairs. Richards stood waiting for them at the bottom.

Some one was opening the front door with a latchkey. It was Brently Mallard who entered, a little travel-stained, composedly carrying his gripsack and umbrella. He had been far from the scene of accident, and did not even know there had been one. He stood amazed at Josephine's piercing cry; at Richards' quick motion to screen him from the view of his wife.

But Richards was too late.

When the doctors came they said she had died of heart disease—of joy that kills.

[1894]

Was their marriage unhappy? Would her friends and family think so? Would her husband have thought so?

Has she become more assertive? Stronger?

Surprising, ironic ending.

STUDENT ESSAY: AN ESSAY THAT COMPARES AND CONTRASTS

Melanie Smith was given the assignment to compare and contrast an element of her choosing in Kate Chopin's "The Story of an Hour" and Charlotte Perkins Gilman's "The Yellow Wallpaper" and to draw some conclusions about life in the nineteenth century. Rather than examining the female protagonists, Melanie chose to focus on the minor male characters in the stories. She wrote a point-by-point comparison designed to demonstrate that these men, despite the opinions of them that she heard expressed in class, were not bad people. Rather, they were led by their social training to behave in ways that were perfectly acceptable in their day, even if they now strike readers as oppressive.

Smith 1

Melanie Smith
Professor Hallet
English 109
17 May 2020

Good Husbands in Bad Marriages

When twenty-first-century readers first encounter literature of earlier times, it is easy for us to apply our own standards of conduct to the characters and situations. Kate Chopin's "The Story of an Hour" and Charlotte Perkins Gilman's "The Yellow Wallpaper" offer two good examples of this. Both written by American women in the last decade of the nineteenth century, the stories give us a look into the lives, and especially the marriages, of middle-class women of the time. By modern standards, the husbands of the two protagonists, particularly John in "The Yellow Wallpaper," seem almost unbearably controlling of their wives. From the vantage point of the late nineteenth century, however, their behavior looks quite different. Both men are essentially well meaning and try to be good husbands. Their only real crime is that they adhere too closely to the conventional Victorian wisdom about women and marriage.

Melanie signals that she will focus on these two stories and makes a claim about them that she will go on to support.

Smith 2

To begin with, both men are well respected in their communities. John in "The Yellow Wallpaper" is described as "a physician of high standing" who has "an intense horror of superstition, and he scoffs openly at any talk of things not to be felt and seen and put down in figures" (85). These are just the qualities that we might expect to find in a respectable doctor, even today. It is less clear what Brently Mallard in "The Story of an Hour" does for a living. (In fact, Chopin's story is so short that we learn fairly little about any of the characters.) But he and his wife seem to live in a comfortable house, and they are surrounded by family and friends, suggesting a secure, well-connected lifestyle. In the nineteenth century, a man's most important job was to take care of his wife and family, and both men in these stories seem to be performing this job very well.

Melanie's first observation about what the male characters have in common.

In addition to providing a comfortable life for them, it also seems that both men love their wives. When she believes her husband has died, Mrs. Mallard thinks of his "kind, tender hands folded in death; the face that had never looked save with love upon her" (100). Her own love for him is less certain, which may be why she feels "free" (101) when he dies, but his love for her seems genuine. The case of John in "The Yellow Wallpaper" is a bit more complicated. To a modern reader, it seems that he treats his wife more like a child than a grown woman. He puts serious restraints on her actions, and at one point he even calls her "little girl" (92). But he also calls her "my darling" and "dear" (92), and she does admit, "He loves me very dearly" (91). When he has to leave her alone, he even has his sister come to look after her, which is a kind gesture, even if it seems a bit like he doesn't trust his wife. If the narrator, who is in a position to know, doesn't doubt her husband's love, what gives us the right to judge it?

A smooth transition into the next point.

To a certain extent, we must admit that both husbands do oppress their wives by being overprotective. Part of the point of both stories is to show how even acceptable, supposedly good marriages of the day could be overly confining to women.

Melanie establishes a similarity between the husbands.

Smith 3

This is especially obvious when we see how much John restricts his wife — forbidding her even to visit her cousins or to write letters — and how everyone expects her to submit to his demands. Though Mrs. Mallard isn't literally confined to a house or a room the way the narrator of "The Yellow Wallpaper" is, she stays inside the house and is looking out the window longingly when she realizes she wants to be free. But it is important for a reader not to blame the husbands, because they really don't intend to be oppressive.

In fact, it is true that both of the wives are in somewhat frail health. Mrs. Mallard is "afflicted with a heart trouble" (99), and the narrator of "The Yellow Wallpaper" seems to have many physical and mental problems, so it is not surprising that their husbands worry about them. It is not evil intent that leads the men to act as they do; it is simply ignorance. John seems less innocent than Brently because he is so patronizing and he puts such restrictions on his wife's behavior and movement, but that kind of attitude was normal for the day, and as a doctor, John seems to be doing what he really thinks is best.

A point of similarity between the wives.

All the other characters in the stories see both men as good and loving husbands, which suggests that society would have approved of their behavior. Even the wives themselves, who are the victims of these oppressive marriages, don't blame the men at all. The narrator of "The Yellow Wallpaper" even thinks she is "ungrateful" (87) for not appreciating John's loving care more. Once we understand this, readers should not be too quick to blame the men either. The real blame falls to the society that gave these men the idea that women are frail and need protection from the world. The men may be the immediate cause of the women's suffering, but the real cause is much deeper and has to do with cultural attitudes and how the men were brought up to protect and provide for women.

Melanie returns to her original claim.

Smith 4

Most people who live in a society don't see the flaws in that society's conventional ways of thinking and living. We now know that women are capable and independent and that protecting them as if they were children ultimately does more harm than good. But in the late Victorian era, such an idea would have seemed either silly or dangerously radical to most people, men and women alike. Stories like these, however, could have helped their original readers begin to think about how confining these supposedly good marriages were. Fortunately, authors such as Chopin and Gilman come along from time to time and show us the problems in our conventional thinking, so society can move forward and we can begin to see how even the most well-meaning actions should sometimes be questioned.

Melanie's conclusion argues for the idea that literature is capable of challenging the status quo.

Works Cited

Chopin, Kate. "The Story of an Hour." *Reading and Writing about Literature: A Portable Guide*, edited by Janet E. Gardner and Joanne Diaz, 5th ed., Bedford/St. Martin's, 2021, pp. 99–101.
Gilman, Charlotte Perkins. "The Yellow Wallpaper." Gardner and Diaz, pp. 85–99.

CHAPTER 6

Writing about Poems

Poetry may be divided into several major subgenres and types. A **narrative poem**, for instance, tells a story. An **epic**, a subgenre of narrative, is a long poem that narrates heroic events. A **lyric poem** expresses the personal thoughts and feelings of a particular poet or speaker. And many other types of poems have venerable histories.

As with stories, you should be aware of certain elements as you prepare to write about poetry. Sometimes these elements are the same as for fiction. A narrative poem, for instance, will have a **plot**, **setting**, and **characters**, and all poems speak from a particular **point of view**. To the extent that any of the elements of fiction help you understand a poem, by all means use them in your analysis. Poetry, however, does present a special set of concerns for a reader, and elements of poetry frequently provide rich ground for analysis.

ELEMENTS OF POETRY

The Speaker

First, consider the speaker of the poem. Imagine that someone is saying the words of this poem aloud. Who is speaking, where is this **speaker**, and what is his or her state of mind? Sometimes, the voice is that of the poet, but frequently a poem speaks from a different perspective, just as a short story might be from a point of view very different from the author's. It's not always apparent when this is the case, but some poets will signal who the speaker is in a title, such as "The Passionate Shepherd to His Love" and "The Love Song of J. Alfred Prufrock" (p. 112). Be alert to signals that will help you recognize the speaker, and remember that some poems have more than one speaker.

The Listener

Be attentive also to any other persons in the poem, particularly an implied listener. Is there a "you" to whom the poem is addressed? If the poem is being spoken aloud, who is supposed to hear it?

106

When, early in his poem "Dover Beach," Matthew Arnold writes, "Come to the window, sweet is the night-air!" he gives us an important clue as to how to read the poem. We should imagine both the speaker and the implied listener together in a room, with a window open to the night. As we read on, we can look for further clues as to who these two people are and why they are together on this night. Many poems create a relationship between the "I" of the speaker and the "you" of the listener; however, that is not always the case. Sometimes the speaker does not address a "you" and instead provides a more philosophical meditation that isn't explicitly addressed to a listener. Consider the effect: Do they feel more abstract? Are they detached from the material conditions of time and place? Do they provide certainty or resolution? The questions about the speaker and the listener are crucial to your analysis of poetry.

Imagery

Just as you should be open to the idea that there are frequently symbols in stories, you should pay special attention to the **images** in poems. Although poems are often about such grand themes as love or death, they rarely dwell long in these abstractions. Rather, the best poetry seeks to make the abstraction concrete by creating vivid images appealing directly to the senses. A well-written poem will provide the mind of an attentive reader with sights, sounds, tastes, scents, and sensations. Isolate these images and give some thought to what they make you think and how they make you feel. Are they typical or unexpected?

Consider the following excerpt from John Donne's "The Good-Morrow":

> My face in thine eye, thine in mine appears,
> And true plain hearts do in the faces rest;
> Where can we find two better hemispheres,
> Without sharp north, without declining west? (lines 15–18)

In the above lines, Donne celebrates the love between the speaker and his object of desire, comparing the faces of the lovers to two "hemispheres" on globes. Elsewhere in the poem, Donne uses imagery that is borrowed from the world of navigation and mapping; here, he suggests that the lovers' faces are an improvement upon whatever instruments explorers and learned men use to understand the world. By examining the images in a poem, their placement, juxtaposition, and effect, you will have gone a long way toward understanding the poem as a whole.

Sound and Sense

Of all the genres, poetry is the one that most self-consciously highlights language, so it is necessary to pay special attention to the sounds of a poem. In fact, it is always a good idea to read a poem aloud several times, giving yourself the opportunity to experience the role that sound plays in the poem's meaning.

Rhyme

Much of the poetry written in English before the twentieth century was written in some form of **rhyme**, and contemporary poets continue to experiment with its effects. Rhymes may seem stilted or old-fashioned to our twenty-first-century ears, but keep in mind that rhymes have powerful social meanings in the cultural context in which they're written. And even today rhyme remains a viable and significant convention in popular songs, which are, after all, a form of poetry. As you read poems, ask yourself how rhymes work. Do they create **juxtapositions**? Alignments of meaning? And what is the effect of that relationship as the poem progresses?

Assonance and Consonance

While it is important to look at the end of a line to see how the poet uses sounds, it is also important to look inside the line. Poets use **assonance**, or repeated vowel sounds, to create an aural effect. Consider the following closing lines from Gerard Manley Hopkins's "God's Grandeur":

> And though the last lights off the black West went
> > Oh, morning, at the brown brink eastward, springs —
> Because the Holy Ghost óver the bent
> > World broods with warm breast and with ah! bright wings. (lines 11–14)

Throughout these lines, Hopkins pays special attention to the "ee" and "oh" sounds. Notice "brink," "eastward," and "springs" in line 12, and then the continuation of the "ee" sound in "wings" in line 14. Notice the word "Oh" in line 12, and then the words "Holy," "Ghost," and "over" in line 13. As you read through each line, ask yourself: Why does the poet align these sounds? Do these sounds speed up the tempo of the line, or slow it down? What do these sounds — and words — reveal about the poet's praise of "God's Grandeur"?

Poets also use **consonance**, repeated consonant sounds, to create alignments and juxtapositions among consonants. Consider these first lines from Christopher Marlowe's "The Passionate Shepherd to His Love":

> Come live with me and be my love,
>
> And we will all the pleasures prove (lines 1–2)

In line 1, Marlowe aligns "live" with "love" to suggest that there is an equation between cohabitation and romance. In line 2, he aligns the *p* sound in "pleasures prove"; in addition, though, the **slant rhyme** of "love" and "prove" also creates meaning between the lines. What "proof" is there in love? Is love what will make the speaker feel most alive?

Meter

Poetry written in English is both **accentual** and **syllabic**. That is, poets count the number of accents as well as the number of syllables as they create each line of poetry. Patterns of syllable and accent have names like *iambic pentameter* and *dactylic tetrameter*, and each meter has its own unique properties and effects. Your literature instructor may help you learn about the specifics of meter, or you can find several sites online that explain the art—called **scansion**—of determining the meter of a poem. Whether or not you have a clear understanding of the many meters of poetry in English, when you read a poem, listen to each line to find out how many accents and syllables it contains. If you can determine what that meter is, consider how the poet uses—and subverts—that formula as part of a strategy for the poem.

Form

Poets writing in English use dozens of traditional forms from a variety of traditions. Some of the most common of these forms are the **sonnet**, the **villanelle**, and the **ballad**, but there are too many to name here. As you read a poem in a traditional form, think of the form as a kind of template in which poets arrange and explore challenging emotional and intellectual material. A sonnet, for example, has a concise fourteen-line structure that allows the poet to address a religious, romantic, or philosophical argument in a very compressed space. As you read a sonnet, you might ask yourself: What does its form accomplish that is different from a longer, more narrative-driven form like a ballad? The two sample poems later in this chapter provide a good opportunity to compare a short, highly conventional form with a longer one.

Note, too, that many contemporary poets write in **free verse**, which means that they don't necessarily use a strict traditional form or meter for their poems. That doesn't mean that the free verse poet is writing without rules; it just means that the poet is creating his or her own system for the unique needs of each poem.

Stanzas

A **stanza** is any grouping of lines of poetry into a unit. The term *stanza* comes from the Italian word for "room." As you read poetry, imagine each stanza as a room with its own correspondences and relationships, and consider how that stanza creates a singular effect. Sometimes a stanza can be one line long; sometimes the poet creates a block of lines with no stanza breaks. All of these choices create distinct effects for readers of poetry.

Lineation

Lineation—or how a poet uses the line breaks in the poem—is a crucial component of poetry. Sometimes poets use punctuation at the ends of lines, but more often they mix end-stopped lines with enjambed lines. **Enjambment** occurs when the line is not end-stopped with a comma, dash, or period. Its meaning spills over onto the next line, creating the effect of acceleration and intensity. Poets also use **caesuras** in the middle of their lines to create variety in the pattern of the line. A caesura is a deep pause created by a comma, colon, semicolon, dash, period, or white space.

TWO POEMS FOR ANALYSIS

Take a few minutes to read William Shakespeare's Sonnet 116 and T. S. Eliot's "The Love Song of J. Alfred Prufrock" and consider the student annotations and the questions that follow the poems. Both of these poems are complex, though in very different ways. What elements of poetry do you notice in these poems? What insights do you have in addition to those suggested by the annotations and questions? (See Questions for Active Reading: Poetry, p. 12.)

WILLIAM SHAKESPEARE   [1564–1616]

Sonnet 116

Let me not to the marriage of true minds   *Consonance: marriage/minds.*
Admit impediments. Love is not love   *Repetition: love/love, alters/*
Which alters when it alteration finds,   *alteration, remover/remove.*
Or bends with the remover to remove.
O, no, it is an ever-fixèd mark   5
That looks on tempests and is never shaken;   *Abstract ideas become specific*
It is the star to every wandering bark,°   *images: tempests, ships.*
Whose worth's unknown, although his height be taken.°
Love's not time's fool, though rosy lips and cheeks   *Rosy lips and cheeks:*
Within his bending sickle's compass come;   *classic love poem images.*
Love alters not with his brief hours and weeks,   10
But bears it out even to the edge of doom.°   *Sickle is a death image,*
  If this be error and upon me proved,   *unusual for a love poem.*
  I never writ, nor no man ever loved.

Final rhyme is slant rhyme.

[1609]

7. **bark:** Ship   8. **taken:** Is measured   12. **doom:** Judgment Day

The student who annotated noticed both structural features of the poem
(such as the move from abstract to concrete language) and small-scale
language features, such as consonance and repetitions of individual
words. This provides a good beginning to understanding the poem;
answering the questions that follow will deepen that understanding,
making it easier to write a paper about the poem.

T. S. ELIOT   [1888–1965]

The Love Song of J. Alfred Prufrock

S'io credesse che mia risposta fosse
A persona che mai tornasse al mondo,
Questa fiamma staria senza piu scosse.
Ma perciocche giammai di questo fondo
Non torno vivo alcun, s'i'odo il vero,
Senza tema d'infamia ti rispondo.

Footnote says this is from Dante's Inferno. *The speaker is in hell. Why start a "love song" with hell?*

Let us go then, you and I,   *Who is this "you"? Where are they going?*
When the evening is spread out against the sky
Like a patient etherised upon a table;
Let us go, through certain half-deserted streets,
The muttering retreats   5
Of restless nights in one-night cheap hotels
And sawdust restaurants with oyster-shells: *Setting grubby and seedy. Depressing.*
Streets that follow like a tedious argument
Of insidious intent
To lead you to an overwhelming question . . .   10
Oh, do not ask, "What is it?"
Let us go and make our visit.   *Who are they visiting? Why?*
     In the room the women come and go   *New setting, in a room. Visiting "the women"?*
Talking of Michelangelo.

     The yellow fog that rubs its back upon the window-panes,   15
The yellow smoke that rubs its muzzle on the window-panes
Licked its tongue into the corners of the evening,   *Fog like an animal,*
Lingered upon the pools that stand in drains,   *almost a character.*
Let fall upon its back the soot that falls from chimneys,
Slipped by the terrace, made a sudden leap,   20
And seeing that it was a soft October night,
Curled once about the house, and fell asleep.   *Uses rhyme in irregular pattern.*

     And indeed there will be time
For the yellow smoke that slides along the street,
Rubbing its back upon the window-panes;   25
There will be time, there will be time   *Lots of repetition here,*
To prepare a face to meet the faces that you meet;   *as if he's fixated on these*
                                                     ideas and can't let go.

There will be time to murder and create,
And time for all the works and days° of hands
That lift and drop a question on your plate;   30
Time for you and time for me,   *He seems obsessed with time*
And time yet for a hundred indecisions,   *and how much of it there is.*
And for a hundred visions and revisions,
Before the taking of a toast and tea.

    In the room the women come and go   *Another repetition. Same women?*   35
Talking of Michelangelo.   *Same room?*

    And indeed there will be time
To wonder, "Do I dare?" and, "Do I dare?"
Time to turn back and descend the stair,
With a bald spot in the middle of my hair—   40
(They will say: "How his hair is growing thin!")   *Physical description:*
My morning coat, my collar mounting firmly to the chin,   *aging, thin, well*
My necktie rich and modest, but asserted by a simple pin—   *dressed. Insecure.*
                                                                Indecisive.

(They will say: "But how his arms and legs are thin!")
Do I dare   45
Disturb the universe?   *How could he "disturb*
                                                      the universe"?

In a minute there is time
For decisions and revisions which a minute will reverse.

    For I have known them all already, known them all:—   *He seems bored*
Have known the evenings, mornings, afternoons,   *with his life.*   50
I have measured out my life with coffee spoons;   *Maybe*
I know the voices dying with a dying fall°   *depressed?*
Beneath the music from a farther room.
    So how should I presume?

    And I have known the eyes already, known them all—   55
The eyes that fix you in a formulated phrase,
And when I am formulated, sprawling on a pin,
When I am pinned and wriggling on the wall,   *Like a bug. More insecurity?*

29. works and days: *Works and Days* is the title of a didactic poem about farming by the Greek poet Hesiod (eighth century B.C.E.) that includes instruction about doing each task at the proper time.

52. a dying fall: An allusion to Shakespeare's *Twelfth Night* (1.1.4): "That strain [of music] again! It had a dying fall" (a cadence that falls away).

Then how should I begin
To spit out all the butt-ends of my days and ways? 60
    And how should I presume?

    And I have known the arms already, known them all—
Arms that are braceleted and white and bare
(But in the lamplight, downed with light brown hair!)
Is it perfume from a dress 65
That makes me so digress?
Arms that lie along a table, or wrap about a shawl.
        And should I then presume? *He asks many questions in this section. Maybe*
        And how should I begin? *unsure of self. Women seem to make him insecure.*

                    •   •   •

Shall I say, I have gone at dusk through narrow streets 70
And watched the smoke that rises from the pipes
Of lonely men in shirt-sleeves, leaning out of windows? . . .
        I should have been a pair of ragged claws *Earlier he was like a*
Scuttling across the floors of silent seas. *bug, now like a crab.*

                    •   •   •

And the afternoon, the evening, sleeps so peacefully! 75
Smoothed by long fingers,
Asleep . . . tired . . . or it malingers,
Stretched on the floor, here beside you and me.
Should I, after tea and cakes and ices,

Have the strength to force the moment to its crisis? 80
But though I have wept and fasted, wept and prayed,
Though I have seen my head (grown slightly bald) brought in upon a
        platter,° *Lots of disconnected body parts:*
                    eyes, arms, claws, head!
I am no prophet—and here's no great matter;
I have seen the moment of my greatness flicker,
And I have seen the eternal Footman hold my coat, and snicker, 85
And in short, I was afraid. *Eternal Footman = Death? Again, he thinks*
                    someone is laughing at him.

---

82. head . . . platter: As a reward for dancing before King Herod, Salome, his
stepdaughter, asked for the head of John the Baptist to be presented to her on a
platter (Matthew 14:1–12; Mark 6:17–28).

And would it have been worth it, after all,
After the cups, the marmalade, the tea,
Among the porcelain, among some talk of you and me,
Would it have been worth while,   90
To have bitten off the matter with a smile,
To have squeezed the universe into a ball
To roll it toward some overwhelming question,
To say: "I am Lazarus,° come from the dead, ——More about death. Who is dead
Come back to tell you all, I shall tell you all" —   here? Prufrock himself?   95
If one, settling a pillow by her head,
    Should say: "That is not what I meant at all.
    That is not it, at all."

Sunsets and teacups seem so much nicer, sweeter than the grim cityscape earlier. Another new setting? How do they connect?

And would it have been worth it, after all,
Would it have been worth while,   100
After the sunsets and the dooryards and the sprinkled streets,
After the novels, after the teacups, after the skirts that trail along the
    floor—
And this, and so much more?—
It is impossible to say just what I mean!
But as if a magic lantern threw the nerves in patterns on a screen: 105
Would it have been worth while
If one, settling a pillow or throwing off a shawl,
And turning toward the window, should say: *Who is repeating this? "That is not*
    "That is not it at all,   *what I meant" = misunderstanding.*
    That is not what I meant, at all."   110

              • • •

No! I am not Prince Hamlet, nor was meant to be;   *Why compare self to*
Am an attendant lord, one that will do   *Hamlet? He's not a*
                                  prince? Not famous?

To swell a progress,° start a scene or two,
Advise the prince; no doubt, an easy tool,
Deferential, glad to be of use,   115
Politic, cautious, and meticulous;

94. Lazarus: Either the beggar Lazarus, who in Luke 16:19–31 did not return
from the dead, or Jesus' friend Lazarus, who did (John 11:1–44).
113. progress: Ceremonial journey made by a royal court.

Full of high sentence, but a bit obtuse;
At times, indeed, almost ridiculous —
Almost, at times, the Fool.

I grow old . . . I grow old . . .   *Worry about aging. How old is he?*   120
I shall wear the bottoms of my trousers rolled.

Shall I part my hair behind? Do I dare to eat a peach?   *A peach? How is*
I shall wear white flannel trousers, and walk upon the beach.   *that daring?*
I have heard the mermaids singing, each to each.

I do not think that they will sing to me.   125

I have seen them riding seaward on the waves   *Setting changes again:*
Combing the white hair of the waves blown back   *now a beach.*
When the wind blows the water white and black.

We have lingered in the chambers of the sea   *Underwater (like the crab*
By sea-girls wreathed with seaweed red and brown   *earlier).*   130
Till human voices wake us, and we drown.   *Wake us? Is this all a dream?*
    A nightmare?

[1915]

On a first reading, the student was baffled by the complexities of this poem and felt certain that it was over her head. After annotating it on a second read through, however, she realized that she had gotten far more out of it than she originally believed and that she had begun to develop some interesting ideas about the speaker and the setting. When her class discussed the poem, she had insightful comments to add to the discussion. The following questions build on and deepen these insights.

STUDENT ESSAY: AN EXPLICATION

Patrick McCorkle, the author of the paper that follows, was given the assignment to perform a close reading of one of the poems his class had studied. He needed first to pick a poem and then to choose specific features of its language to isolate and analyze. He chose Shakespeare's Sonnet 116 (p. 111) because it seemed to him to offer an interesting and balanced definition of love. After rereading the poem, he became interested in several unexpectedly negative, even unsettling images that seemed out of place in a poem about the positive emotion of love.

Patrick McCorkle

Professor Bobrick

English 102

10 January 2020

Shakespeare Defines Love

From the earliest written rhymes to the latest radio hit, love is among the eternal themes for poetry. Most love poetry seems to fall into one of two categories. Either the poet sings the praises of the beloved and the unending joys of love in overly exaggerated terms, or the poet laments the loss of love with such bitterness and distress that it seems like the end of life. Anyone who has been in love, though, can tell you that both of these views are limited and incomplete and that real love is neither entirely joyous nor entirely sad. In Sonnet 116, "Let me not to the marriage of true minds," Shakespeare creates a more realistic image of love. By balancing negative with positive images and language, this sonnet does a far better job than thousands of songs and poems before and since, defining love in all its complexities and contradictions.

Patrick identifies his topic and states his thesis.

Like many poems, Sonnet 116 relies on a series of visual images to paint vivid pictures for the reader, but not all of these images are what we might expect in a poem celebrating the pleasures of lasting love. A reader can easily picture "an ever-fixèd mark" (line 5), a "tempest," a "star," a "wandering bark" (a boat lost at sea) (6–7), "rosy lips and cheeks" (8), and a "bending sickle" (9). Some of these, like stars and rosy lips, are just the sort of sunny, positive images we typically find in love poems of the joyous variety. Others, though, are more unexpected. Flowers and images of springtime, for instance, are standard issue in happy love poetry, but a sickle is associated with autumn and the death of the year, and metaphorically with death itself in the form of the grim reaper. Likewise, a boat tossed in a raging tempest is not exactly the typical poetic depiction of happy love.

Patrick introduces the poem's contradictory imagery.

Such pictures would hardly seem to provide an upbeat image of what love is all about, and in fact they might be more at home

Patrick explains the effect of this imagery.

in one of the sad poems about the loss of love. But these tempests and sickles are more realistic than the hearts and flowers of so many lesser love poems. In fact, they show that the poet recognizes the bad times that occur in all relationships, even those strong enough to inspire love sonnets. And the negative images are tempered because of the contexts in which they occur. The "wandering bark," for instance, might represent trouble and loss, but love itself is seen as the star that will lead the boat safely back to calm waters. Meanwhile, the beloved's "rosy lips and cheeks" may fade, but real love outlives even the stroke of death's sickle, lasting "to the edge of doom" (12).

Just as positive and negative images are juxtaposed, so are positive and negative language. The first four lines of Sonnet 116 are made up of two sentences, both negatives, beginning with the words "Let me not" and "Love is not." The negatives of the first few lines continue in phrases like "Whose worth's unknown" (8) and "Love's not time's fool" (9). From here, the poem goes on to dwell in abstract ideas such as "alteration" (3), "impediments" (2), and "error" (13). None of this is what readers of love poems have been led to expect in their previous reading, and we might even wonder if the poet finds this love thing worth the trouble. This strange and unexpected language continues on through the last line of the poem, which contains no fewer than three negative words: "never," "nor," and "no."

Patrick integrates direct quotations from the poem into his close reading.

Where, a reader might ask, are the expected positive descriptions of love? Where are the summer skies, the smiles and laughter? Clearly, Shakespeare doesn't mean to sweep his readers up in rosy images of a lover's bliss. Ultimately, though, even with the preponderance of negative images and words, the poem strikes a hopeful tone. The hedging about what love isn't and what it can't do are balanced with positive words and phrases, saying clearly what love is: "it is an ever-fixèd mark" (5) and "it is the star" (7). Love, it would seem, does not make our lives perfect, but it gives us the strength, stability, and direction to survive the bad times.

McCorkle 3

Though more than four hundred years have passed since Shakespeare wrote his sonnets, some things never change, and among these is the nature of complex human emotions. In a mere fourteen lines, Shakespeare succeeds where many others have failed through the years, providing a much more satisfying definition of love than one normally sees in one-dimensional, strictly happy or sad poetry. The love he describes is the sort that not everyone is lucky enough to find — a "marriage of true minds" — complicated, unsettling, and very real.

In his conclusion, Patrick suggests that the poem is successful because of the juxtapositions he has discussed.

Work Cited

Shakespeare, William. "Sonnet 116." *Reading and Writing about Literature: A Portable Guide*, edited by Janet E. Gardner and Joanne Diaz, 5th ed., Bedford/St. Martin's, 2021, p. 111.

CHAPTER 7

Writing about Plays

Perhaps the earliest literary critic in the Western tradition was Aristotle, who, in the fifth century B.C.E., set about explaining the power of the genre of **tragedy** by identifying the six **elements of drama** and analyzing the contribution each of these elements makes to the functioning of a play as a whole. The elements that Aristotle identified as common to all dramas were plot, characterization, theme, diction, melody, and spectacle. Some of these are the same as or very similar to the basic components of prose fiction and poetry, but others are either unique to drama or expressed differently in dramatic texts. (See Questions for Active Reading: Drama, p. 14.)

ELEMENTS OF DRAMA

Plot, Character, and Theme

The words *plot*, *character*, and *theme* mean basically the same thing in drama as they do in fiction, though there is a difference in how they are presented. A story *tells* you about a series of events, whereas a play *shows* you these events happening in real time. The information that might be conveyed in descriptive passages in prose fiction must be conveyed in a play through **dialogue** (and to a lesser extent through **stage directions** and the **set** and character descriptions that sometimes occur at the start of a play). The "How to Read a Play" section later in this chapter gives suggestions and advice for understanding these special features of drama.

Diction

When Aristotle speaks of **diction**, he means the specific words that a playwright chooses to put into the mouth of a character. In a well-written play, different characters will have different ways of speaking, and these will tell us a good deal about their character and personality. Does one character sound very formal and well educated? Does another speak in slang or dialect? Does someone hesitate or speak in fits and starts, perhaps indicating distraction or nervousness? Practice paying attention to these nuances. And keep in mind that just because a character says something, that doesn't make it true. As in real life, some characters might be mistaken in what they say, or they may be hiding the truth or even telling outright lies.

Spectacle

Spectacle refers to what we actually see onstage when we go to a play — the costumes, the actors' movements, the sets, the lights, and so forth. All of these details make a difference in how we understand and interpret a play's message. Hamlet's famous "To be or not to be" soliloquy will resonate differently with an audience if the actor playing Hamlet is wearing ripped jeans and a T-shirt, or a modern military uniform, rather than the conventional Renaissance doublet and hose. When reading a play, it is important to remember that it was not written to be read only, but rather so that it would be seen onstage in the communal setting of a theater. Reading with this in mind and trying to imagine the spectacle of a real production will increase your enjoyment of plays immensely. Specific suggestions for this sort of reading can be found in the "How to Read a Play" section of this chapter.

Setting

A **setting**, which Aristotle ignores completely, is just as important in drama as it is in fiction. But again, in drama it must be either displayed onstage or alluded to through the characters' words rather than being described as it might be in a story or a poem. The texts of modern plays often (though not always) begin with elaborate descriptions of the stage, furniture, major props, and so forth, which can be very useful in helping you picture a production. These tend to be absent in older plays, so in some cases you will have to use your imagination to fill in these gaps. In act 4 of *Hamlet*, the characters are in a castle one moment and on a windswept plain the next. The only way a reader can be aware of this shift, though, is by paying close attention to the words and actions that characters use to signal a change of locale.

HOW TO READ A PLAY

Very few of us read plays for pleasure in the same way that we might take a novel with us to the beach. This isn't surprising: most playwrights, in fact, never intend for their plays to be read in this way. Drama is a living art, and if you read the play text on the page, you are getting only one part of what has made drama so important to all cultures across many time periods. Plays are written for the stage and are meant to be experienced primarily in live performance. This means that as a reader you must be especially attentive to nuances of language in a play, which often means imagining what might be happening onstage during a particular passage of speech. Using your imagination in this way — in effect, staging the play in your mind — will help you with some of the difficulties inherent in reading plays.

Watching the Play

If you have access to a film version of the play that you are examining, be sure to watch it. Do bear in mind, though, that play scripts usually undergo substantial rewriting to adapt them for film, so you will still need to read the play in its original form, perhaps making comparisons between the stage and film versions. If you are reading a Shakespeare play, you can usually choose from several film versions, many of which might be in your library's collection. Live drama, of course, is different from film. Check the listings of local theaters to see what they are staging; you might find that a theater company is performing the play that you have to read for your class.

The Director's Vision

Some of the most skilled readers of plays are theater directors. These professionals have developed the ability to read a play and instantly see and hear in their minds the many possibilities for how the play might look and sound onstage. Directors understand that a play script is just one piece of a large, collaborative process involving playwright, director, designers, actors, backstage crew, and audience. Every new production of a play is different — sometimes vastly different — from the productions that have gone before, and every play script yields nearly endless possibilities for creative staging. By altering the look and feel of a play, a director puts his or her individual stamp on it, connecting with the audience in a unique way and helping that audience understand the playwright's and the director's messages. The questions that follow are the sort that a director would consider when reading a play. As you read plays for your literature class, these questions can help you formulate a consistent and strong interpretation.

SUSAN GLASPELL   [1882–1948]

Trifles

Characters

GEORGE HENDERSON, *county attorney*
HENRY PETERS, *sheriff*
LEWIS HALE, *a neighboring farmer*
MRS. PETERS
MRS. HALE

Scene: The kitchen in the now abandoned farmhouse of John Wright, a gloomy kitchen, and left without having been put in order—the walls covered with a faded wall paper. Down right is a door leading to the parlor. On the right wall above this door is a built-in kitchen cupboard with shelves in the upper portion and drawers below. In the rear wall at right, up two steps is a door opening onto stairs leading to the second floor. In the rear wall at left is a door to the shed and from there to the outside. Between these two doors is an old-fashioned black iron stove. Running along the left wall from the shed door is an old iron sink and sink shelf, in which is set a hand pump. Downstage of the sink is an uncurtained window. Near the window is an old wooden rocker. Center stage is an unpainted wooden kitchen table with straight chairs on either side. There is a small chair down right. Unwashed pans under the sink, a loaf of bread outside the breadbox, a dish towel on the table—other signs of incompleted work. At the rear the shed door opens and the Sheriff comes in followed by the County Attorney and Hale. The Sheriff and Hale are men in middle life, the County Attorney is a young man; all are much bundled up and go at once to the stove. They are followed by the two women—the Sheriff's wife, Mrs. Peters, first: she is a slight wiry woman, a thin nervous face. Mrs. Hale is larger and would ordinarily be called more comfortable looking, but she is disturbed now and looks fearfully about as she enters. The women have come in slowly, and stand close together near the door.

COUNTY ATTORNEY (*at stove rubbing his hands*): This feels good. Come up to the fire, ladies.

MRS. PETERS (*after taking a step forward*): I'm not—cold.

SHERIFF (*unbuttoning his overcoat and stepping away from the stove to right of table as if to mark the beginning of official business*): Now, Mr. Hale, before we move things about, you explain to Mr. Henderson just what you saw when you came here yesterday morning.

COUNTY ATTORNEY (*crossing down to left of the table*): By the way, has anything been moved? Are things just as you left them yesterday?

123

SHERIFF (*looking about*): It's just about the same. When it dropped below zero last night I thought I'd better send Frank out this morning to make a fire for us—(*sits right of center table*) no use getting pneumonia with a big case on, but I told him not to touch anything except the stove—and you know Frank.

COUNTY ATTORNEY: Somebody should have been left here yesterday.

SHERIFF: Oh—yesterday. When I had to send Frank to Morris Center for that man who went crazy—I want you to know I had my hands full yesterday. I knew you could get back from Omaha by today and as long as I went over everything here myself——

COUNTY ATTORNEY: Well, Mr. Hale, tell just what happened when you came here yesterday morning.

HALE (*crossing down to above table*): Harry and I had started to town with a load of potatoes. We came along the road from my place and as I got here I said, "I'm going to see if I can't get John Wright to go in with me on a party telephone." I spoke to Wright about it once before and he put me off, saying folks talked too much anyway, and all he asked was peace and quiet—I guess you know about how much he talked himself; but I thought maybe if I went to the house and talked about it before his wife, though I said to Harry that I didn't know as what his wife wanted made much difference to John——

COUNTY ATTORNEY: Let's talk about that later, Mr. Hale. I do want to talk about that, but tell now just what happened when you got to the house.

HALE: I didn't hear or see anything; I knocked at the door, and still it was all quiet inside. I knew they must be up, it was past eight o'clock. So I knocked again, and I thought I heard someone say, "Come in." I wasn't sure, I'm not sure yet, but I opened the door—this door (*indicating the door by which the two women are still standing*) and there in that rocker—(*pointing to it*) sat Mrs. Wright. (*They all look at the rocker down left.*)

COUNTY ATTORNEY: What—was she doing?

HALE: She was rockin' back and forth. She had her apron in her hand and was kind of—pleating it.

COUNTY ATTORNEY: And how did she—look?

HALE: Well, she looked queer.

COUNTY ATTORNEY: How do you mean—queer?

HALE: Well, as if she didn't know what she was going to do next. And kind of done up.

COUNTY ATTORNEY (*takes out notebook and pencil and sits left of center table*): How did she seem to feel about your coming?

HALE: Why, I don't think she minded—one way or other. She didn't pay much attention. I said, "How do, Mrs. Wright, it's cold, ain't it?" And she said, "Is it?"—and went on kind of pleating at her apron. Well, I was surprised: she didn't ask me to come up to the stove, or to set down, but just sat there, not even looking at me, so I said, "I want to see John." And then she—laughed. I guess you would call it a laugh. I thought of Harry and the team outside, so I said a little sharp: "Can't I see John?" "No," she says, kind o' dull like. "Ain't he home?" says I. "Yes," says she, "he's home." "Then why can't I see him?" I asked her, out of patience. "'Cause he's dead," says she. *"Dead?"* says I. She just nodded her head, not getting a bit excited, but rockin' back and forth. "Why—where is he?" says I, not knowing what to say. She just pointed upstairs—like that. (*Himself pointing to the room above.*) I started for the stairs, with the idea of going up there. I walked from there to here—then I says, "Why, what did he die of?" "He died of a rope round his neck," says she, and just went on pleatin' at her apron. Well, I went out and called Harry. I thought I might—need help. We went upstairs and there he was lyin'———

COUNTY ATTORNEY: I think I'd rather have you go into that upstairs, where you can point it all out. Just go on now with the rest of the story.

HALE: Well, my first thought was to get that rope off. It looked . . . (*stops: his face twitches*) . . . but Harry, he went up to him, and he said, "No, he's dead all right, and we'd better not touch anything." So we went right back downstairs. She was still sitting that same way. "Has anybody been notified?" I asked. "No," says she, unconcerned. "Who did this, Mrs. Wright?" said Harry. He said it businesslike—and she stopped pleatin' of her apron. "I don't know," she says. "You don't *know*?" says Harry. "No," says she. "Weren't you sleepin' in the bed with him?" says Harry. "Yes," says she, "but I was on the inside." "Somebody slipped a rope round his head and strangled him and you didn't wake up?" says Harry. "I didn't wake up," she said after him. We must 'a' looked as if we didn't see how that could be, for after a minute she said, "I sleep sound." Harry was going to ask her more questions but I said maybe we ought to let her tell her story first to the coroner, or the sheriff, so Harry went fast as he could to Rivers' place, where there's a telephone.

COUNTY ATTORNEY: And what did Mrs. Wright do when she knew that you had gone for the coroner?

HALE: She moved from the rocker to that chair over there (*pointing to a small chair in the down right corner*) and just sat there with her hands held together and looking down. I got a feeling that I ought to make some conversation, so I said I had come in to see if John wanted to put in a telephone, and at that she started to laugh, and then she stopped and looked at me—scared. (*The County Attorney, who has had his notebook out, makes a note.*) I dunno, maybe it wasn't scared. I wouldn't like to say it was. Soon Harry got back, and then Dr. Lloyd came and you, Mr. Peters, and so I guess that's all I know that you don't.

COUNTY ATTORNEY (*rising and looking around*): I guess we'll go upstairs first—and then out to the barn and around there. (*To the Sheriff.*) You're convinced that there was nothing important here—nothing that would point to any motive?

SHERIFF: Nothing here but kitchen things. (*The County Attorney, after again looking around the kitchen, opens the door of a cupboard closet in right wall. He brings a small chair from right—gets on it and looks on a shelf. Pulls his hand away, sticky.*)

COUNTY ATTORNEY: Here's a nice mess. (*The women draw nearer up to center.*)

MRS. PETERS (*to the other woman*): Oh, her fruit; it did freeze. (*To the Lawyer.*) She worried about that when it turned so cold. She said the fire'd go out and her jars would break.

SHERIFF (*rises*): Well, can you beat the woman! Held for murder and worryin' about her preserves.

COUNTY ATTORNEY (*getting down from chair*): I guess before we're through she may have something more serious than preserves to worry about. (*Crosses down right center.*)

HALE: Well, women are used to worrying over trifles. (*The two women move a little closer together.*)

COUNTY ATTORNEY (*with the gallantry of a young politician*): And yet, for all their worries, what would we do without the ladies? (*The women do not unbend. He goes below the center table to the sink, takes a dipperful of water from the pail, and pouring it into a basin, washes his hands. While he is doing this the Sheriff and Hale cross to cupboard, which they inspect. The County Attorney starts to wipe his hands on the roller towel, turns it for a cleaner place.*) Dirty towels! (*Kicks his foot against the pans under the sink.*) Not much of a housekeeper, would you say, ladies?

MRS. HALE (*stiffly*): There's a great deal of work to be done on a farm.

COUNTY ATTORNEY: To be sure. And yet (*with a little bow to her*) I know there are some Dickson County farmhouses which do not have such roller towels. (*He gives it a pull to expose its full-length again.*)

MRS. HALE: Those towels get dirty awful quick. Men's hands aren't always clean as they might be.

COUNTY ATTORNEY: Ah, loyal to your sex, I see. But you and Mrs. Wright were neighbors. I suppose you were friends, too.

MRS. HALE (*shaking her head*): I've not seen much of her of late years. I've not been in this house—it's more than a year.

COUNTY ATTORNEY (*crossing to women up center*): And why was that? You didn't like her?

MRS. HALE: I liked her all well enough. Farmer's wives have their hands full, Mr. Henderson. And then——

COUNTY ATTORNEY: Yes——?

MRS. HALE (*looking about*): It never seemed a very cheerful place.

COUNTY ATTORNEY: No—it's not cheerful. I shouldn't say she had the homemaking instinct.

MRS. HALE: Well, I don't know as Wright had, either.

COUNTY ATTORNEY: You mean that they didn't get on very well?

MRS. HALE: No, I don't mean anything. But I don't think a place'd be any cheerfuller for John Wright's being in it.

COUNTY ATTORNEY: I'd like to talk more of that a little later. I want to get the lay of things upstairs now. (*He goes past the women to up right where the steps lead to a stair door.*)

SHERIFF: I suppose anything Mrs. Peters does'll be all right. She was to take in some clothes for her, you know, and a few little things. We left in such a hurry yesterday.

COUNTY ATTORNEY: Yes, but I would like to see what you take, Mrs. Peters, and keep an eye out for anything that might be of use to us.

MRS. PETERS: Yes, Mr. Henderson. (*The men leave by up right door to stairs. The women listen to the men's steps on the stairs, then look about the kitchen.*)

MRS. HALE (*crossing left to sink*): I'd hate to have men coming into my kitchen, snooping around and criticizing. (*She arranges the pans under sink which the lawyer had shoved out of place.*)

MRS. PETERS: Of course it's no more than their duty. (*Crosses to cupboard up right.*)

MRS. HALE: Duty's all right, but I guess that deputy sheriff that came out to make the fire might have got a little of this on. (*Gives the roller towel a pull.*) Wish I'd thought of that sooner. Seems mean to talk about her for not having things slicked up when she had to come away in such a hurry. (*Crosses right to Mrs. Peters at cupboard.*)

MRS. PETERS (*who has been looking through cupboard, lifts one end of towel that covers a pan*): She had bread set. (*Stands still.*)

MRS. HALE (*eyes fixed on a loaf of bread beside the breadbox, which is on a low shelf of the cupboard*): She was going to put this in there. (*Picks up loaf, abruptly drops it. In a manner of returning to familiar things.*) It's a shame about her fruit. I wonder if it's all gone. (*Gets up on chair and looks.*) I think there's some here that's all right, Mrs. Peters. Yes—here; (*holding it toward the window*) this is cherries, too. (*Looking again.*) I declare I believe that's the only one. (*Gets down, jar in hand. Goes to the sink and wipes it off on the outside.*) She'll feel awful bad after all her hard work in the hot weather. I remember the afternoon I put up my cherries last summer. (*She puts the jar on the big kitchen table, center of the room. With a sigh, is about to sit down in the rocking chair. Before she is seated realizes what chair it is; with a slow look at it, steps back. The chair which she has touched rocks back and forth. Mrs. Peters moves to center table and they both watch the chair rock for a moment or two.*)

MRS. PETERS (*shaking off the mood which the empty rocking chair has evoked. Now in a businesslike manner she speaks*): Well I must get those things from the front room closet. (*She goes to the door at the right but, after looking into the other room, steps back.*) You coming with me, Mrs. Hale? You could help me carry them. (*They go in the other room; reappear, Mrs. Peters carrying a dress, petticoat, and skirt, Mrs. Hale following with a pair of shoes.*) My, it's cold in there. (*She puts the clothes on the big table and hurries to the stove.*)

MRS. HALE (*right of center table examining the skirt*): Wright was close. I think maybe that's why she kept so much to herself. She didn't even belong to the Ladies' Aid. I suppose she felt she couldn't do her part, and then you don't enjoy things when you feel shabby. I heard she used to wear pretty clothes and be lively, when she was Minnie Foster, one of the town girls singing in the choir. But that—oh, that was thirty years ago. This all you want to take in?

MRS. PETERS: She said she wanted an apron. Funny thing to want, for there isn't much to get you dirty in jail, goodness knows. But I suppose just to make her feel more natural. (*Crosses to cupboard.*) She said they was in the top drawer in this cupboard. Yes, here. And then her little shawl that always hung behind the door. (*Opens stair door and looks.*) Yes, here it is. (*Quickly shuts door leading upstairs.*)

MRS. HALE (*abruptly moving toward her*): Mrs. Peters?

MRS. PETERS: Yes, Mrs. Hale? (*At up right door.*)

MRS. HALE: Do you think she did it?

MRS. PETERS (*in a frightened voice*): Oh, I don't know.

MRS. HALE: Well, I don't think she did. Asking for an apron and her little shawl. Worrying about her fruit.

MRS. PETERS (*starts to speak, glances up, where footsteps are heard in the room above. In a low voice*): Mr. Peters says it looks bad for her. Mr. Henderson is awful sarcastic in a speech and he'll make fun of her sayin' she didn't wake up.

MRS. HALE: Well, I guess John Wright didn't wake when they was slipping that rope under his neck.

MRS. PETERS (*crossing slowly to table and placing shawl and apron on table with other clothing*): No, it's strange. It must have been done awful crafty and still. They say it was such a—funny way to kill a man, rigging it all up like that.

MRS. HALE (*crossing to left of Mrs. Peters at table*): That's just what Mr. Hale said. There was a gun in the house. He says that's what he can't understand.

MRS. PETERS: Mr. Henderson said coming out that what was needed for the case was a motive: something to show anger, or—sudden feeling.

MRS. HALE (*who is standing by the table*): Well, I don't see any signs of anger around here. (*She puts her hand on the dish towel, which lies on the table, stands looking down at table, one-half of which is clean, the other half messy.*) It's wiped to here. (*Makes a move as if to finish work, then turns and looks at loaf of bread outside the breadbox. Drops towel. In that voice of coming back to familiar things.*) Wonder how they are finding things upstairs. (*Crossing below table to down right.*) I hope she had it a little more red-up up there. You know, it seems kind of *sneaking*. Locking her up in town and then coming out here and trying to get her own house to turn against her!

MRS. PETERS: But, Mrs. Hale, the law is the law.

MRS. HALE: I s'pose 'tis. (*Unbuttoning her coat.*) Better loosen up your things, Mrs. Peters. You won't feel them when you go out. (*Mrs. Peters takes off her fur tippet, goes to hang it on chair back left of table, stands looking at the work basket on floor near down left window.*)

MRS. PETERS: She was piecing a quilt. (*She brings the large sewing basket to the center table and they look at the bright pieces, Mrs. Hale above the table and Mrs. Peters left of it.*)

MRS. HALE: It's a log cabin pattern. Pretty, isn't it? I wonder if she was goin' to quilt it or just knot it? (*Footsteps have been heard coming down the stairs. The Sheriff enters followed by Hale and the County Attorney.*)

SHERIFF: They wonder if she was going to quilt it or just knot it! (*The men laugh, the women look abashed.*)

COUNTY ATTORNEY (*rubbing his hands over the stove*): Frank's fire didn't do much up there, did it? Well, let's go out to the barn and get that cleared up. (*The men go outside by up left door.*)

MRS. HALE (*resentfully*): I don't know as there's anything so strange, our takin' up our time with little things while we're waiting for them to get the evidence. (*She sits in chair right of table smoothing out a block with decision.*) I don't see as it's anything to laugh about.

MRS. PETERS (*apologetically*): Of course they've got awful important things on their minds. (*Pulls up a chair and joins Mrs. Hale at the left of the table.*)

MRS. HALE (*examining another block*): Mrs. Peters, look at this one. Here, this is the one she was working on, and look at the sewing! All the rest of it has been so nice and even. And look at this! It's all over the place! Why, it looks as if she didn't know what she was about! (*After she has said this they look at each other, then start to glance back at the door. After an instant Mrs. Hale has pulled at a knot and ripped the sewing.*)

MRS. PETERS: Oh, what are you doing, Mrs. Hale?

MRS. HALE (*mildly*): Just pulling out a stitch or two that's not sewed very good. (*Threading a needle.*) Bad sewing always made me fidgety.

MRS. PETERS (*with a glance at the door, nervously*): I don't think we ought to touch things.

MRS. HALE: I'll just finish up this end. (*Suddenly stopping and leaning forward.*) Mrs. Peters?

MRS. PETERS: Yes, Mrs. Hale?

MRS. HALE: What do you suppose she was so nervous about?

MRS. PETERS: Oh—I don't know. I don't know as she was nervous. I sometimes sew awful queer when I'm just tired. (*Mrs. Hale starts to say something, looks at Mrs. Peters, then goes on sewing.*) Well, I must get these things wrapped up. They may be through sooner than we think. (*Putting apron and other things together.*) I wonder where I can find a piece of paper, and string. (*Rises.*)

MRS. HALE: In that cupboard, maybe.

MRS. PETERS (*crosses right looking in cupboard*): Why, here's a bird-cage. (*Holds it up.*) Did she have a bird, Mrs. Hale?

MRS. HALE: Why, I don't know whether she did or not—I've not been here for so long. There was a man around last year selling canaries cheap, but I don't know as she took one; maybe she did. She used to sing real pretty herself.

MRS. PETERS (*glancing around*): Seems funny to think of a bird here. But she must have had one, or why would she have a cage? I wonder what happened to it?

MRS. HALE: I s'pose maybe the cat got it.

MRS. PETERS: No, she didn't have a cat. She's got that feeling some people have about cats—being afraid of them. My cat got in her room and she was real upset and asked me to take it out.

MRS. HALE: My sister Bessie was like that. Queer, ain't it?

MRS. PETERS (*examining the cage*): Why, look at this door. It's broke. One hinge is pulled apart. (*Takes a step down to Mrs. Hale's right.*)

MRS. HALE (*looking too*): Looks as if someone must have been rough with it.

MRS. PETERS: Why, yes. (*She brings the cage forward and puts it on the table.*)

MRS. HALE (*glancing toward up left door*): I wish if they're going to find any evidence they'd be about it. I don't like this place.

MRS. PETERS: But I'm awful glad you came with me, Mrs. Hale. It would be lonesome for me sitting here alone.

MRS. HALE: It would, wouldn't it? (*Dropping her sewing.*) But I tell you what I do wish, Mrs. Peters. I wish I had come over sometimes when she was here. I—(*looking around the room*)—wish I had.

MRS. PETERS: But of course you were awful busy, Mrs. Hale—your house and your children.

MRS. HALE (*rises and crosses left*): I could've come. I stayed away because it weren't cheerful—and that's why I ought to have come. I—(*looking out left window*)—I've never liked this place. Maybe it's because it's down in a hollow and you don't see the road. I dunno what it is, but it's

a lonesome place and always was. I wish I had come over to see Minnie
Foster sometimes. I can see now—(*Shakes her head.*)

MRS. PETERS (*left of table and above it*): Well, you mustn't reproach yourself, Mrs. Hale. Somehow we just don't see how it is with other folks
until—something turns up.

MRS. HALE: Not having children makes less work—but it makes a quiet
house, and Wright out to work all day, and no company when he did come
in. (*Turning from window.*) Did you know John Wright, Mrs. Peters?

MRS. PETERS: Not to know him; I've seen him in town. They say he was a
good man.

MRS. HALE: Yes—good; he didn't drink, and kept his word as well as
most, I guess, and paid his debts. But he was a hard man, Mrs. Peters.
Just to pass the time of day with him—(*Shivers.*) Like a raw wind that
gets to the bone. (*Pauses, her eye falling on the cage.*) I should think she
would 'a' wanted a bird. But what do you suppose went with it?

MRS. PETERS: I don't know, unless it got sick and died. (*She reaches over
and swings the broken door, swings it again, both women watch it.*)

MRS. HALE: You weren't raised round here, were you? (*Mrs. Peters shakes
her head.*) You didn't know—her?

MRS. PETERS: Not till they brought her yesterday.

MRS. HALE: She—come to think of it, she was kind of like a bird herself—
real sweet and pretty, but kind of timid and—fluttery.
How—she—did—change. (*Silence: then as if struck by a happy thought
and relieved to get back to everyday things. Crosses right above Mrs. Peters to
cupboard, replaces small chair used to stand on to its original place down
right.*) Tell you what, Mrs. Peters, why don't you take the quilt in with
you? It might take up her mind.

MRS. PETERS: Why, I think that's a real nice idea, Mrs. Hale. There couldn't
possibly be any objection to it could there? Now, just what would I
take? I wonder if her patches are in here—and her things. (*They look in
the sewing basket.*)

MRS. HALE (*crosses to right of table*): Here's some red. I expect this has got
sewing things in it. (*Brings out a fancy box.*) What a pretty box. Looks
like something somebody would give you. Maybe her scissors are
in here. (*Opens box. **Suddenly puts her hand** to her nose.*) Why———
(*Mrs. Peters bends nearer, then turns her face away.*) There's something
wrapped up in this piece of silk.

MRS. PETERS: Why, this isn't her scissors.

MRS. HALE (*lifting the silk*): Oh, Mrs. Peters—it's———(*Mrs. Peters bends
closer.*)

MRS. PETERS: It's the bird.

MRS. HALE: But, Mrs. Peters—look at it! Its neck! Look at its neck! It's
all—other side *to*.

MRS. PETERS: Somebody—wrung—its—neck. (*Their eyes meet. A look of growing comprehension, of horror. Steps are heard outside. Mrs. Hale slips box under quilt pieces, and sinks into her chair. Enter Sheriff and County Attorney. Mrs. Peters steps down left and stands looking out of window.*)

COUNTY ATTORNEY (*as one turning from serious things to little pleasantries*): Well, ladies, have you decided whether she was going to quilt it or knot it? (*Crosses to center above table.*)

MRS. PETERS: We think she was going to—knot it. (*Sheriff crosses to right of stove, lifts stove lid, and glances at fire, then stands warming hands at stove.*)

COUNTY ATTORNEY: Well, that's interesting, I'm sure. (*Seeing the bird-cage.*) Has the bird flown?

MRS. HALE (*putting more quilt pieces over the box*): We think the—cat got it.

COUNTY ATTORNEY (*preoccupied*): Is there a cat? (*Mrs. Hale glances in a quick covert way at Mrs. Peters.*)

MRS. PETERS (*turning from window takes a step in*): Well, not *now*. They're superstitious, you know. They leave.

COUNTY ATTORNEY (*to Sheriff Peters, continuing an interrupted conversation*): No sign at all of anyone having come from the outside. Their own rope. Now let's go up again and go over it piece by piece. (*They start upstairs.*) It would have to have been someone who knew just the———(*Mrs. Peters sits down left of table. The two women sit there not looking at one another, but as if peering into something and at the same time holding back. When they talk now it is in the manner of feeling their way over strange ground, as if afraid of what they are saying, but as if they cannot help saying it.*)

MRS. HALE (*hesitatively and in hushed voice*): She liked the bird. She was going to bury it in that pretty box.

MRS. PETERS (*in a whisper*): When I was a girl—my kitten—there was a boy took a hatchet, and before my eyes—and before I could get there———(*Covers her face an instant.*) If they hadn't held me back I would have—(*catches herself, looks upstairs where steps are heard, falters weakly*)—hurt him.

MRS. HALE (*with a slow look around her*): I wonder how it would seem never to have had any children around. (*Pause.*) No, Wright wouldn't like the bird—a thing that sang. She used to sing. He killed that, too.

MRS. PETERS (*moving uneasily*): We don't know who killed the bird.

MRS. HALE: I knew John Wright.

MRS. PETERS: It was an awful thing was done in this house that night, Mrs. Hale. Killing a man while he slept, slipping a rope around his neck that choked the life out of him.

MRS. HALE: His neck. Choked the life out of him. (*Her hand goes out and rests on the bird-cage.*)

MRS. PETERS (*with rising voice*): We don't know who killed him. We don't know.

MRS. HALE (*her own feelings not interrupted*): If there'd been years and years of nothing, then a bird to sing to you, it would be awful—still, after the bird was still.

MRS. PETERS (*something within her speaking*): I know what stillness is. When we homesteaded in Dakota, and my first baby died—after he was two years old, and me with no other then——

MRS. HALE (*moving*): How soon do you suppose they'll be through looking for the evidence?

MRS. PETERS: I know what stillness is. (*Pulling herself back.*) The law has got to punish crimes, Mrs. Hale.

MRS. HALE (*not as if answering that*): I wish you'd seen Minnie Foster when she wore a white dress with blue ribbons and stood up there in the choir and sang. (*A look around the room.*) Oh, I *wish* I'd come over here once in a while! That was a crime! That was a crime! Who's going to punish that?

MRS. PETERS (*looking upstairs*): We mustn't—take on.

MRS. HALE: I might have known she needed help! I know how things can be—for women. I tell you, it's queer, Mrs. Peters. We live close together and we live far apart. We all go through the same things—it's all just a different kind of the same thing. (*Brushes her eyes, noticing the jar of fruit, reaches out for it.*) If I was you I wouldn't tell her her fruit was gone. Tell her it ain't. Tell her it's all right. Take this in to prove it to her. She—she may never know whether it was broke or not.

MRS. PETERS (*takes the jar, looks about for something to wrap it in; takes petticoat from the clothes brought from the other room, very nervously begins winding this around the jar. In a false voice*): My, it's a good thing the men couldn't hear us. Wouldn't they just laugh! Getting all stirred up over a little thing like a—dead canary. As if that could have anything to do with—with—wouldn't they *laugh*! (*The men are heard coming downstairs.*)

MRS. HALE (*under her breath*): Maybe they would—maybe they wouldn't.

COUNTY ATTORNEY: No, Peters, it's all perfectly clear except a reason for doing it. But you know juries when it comes to women. If there was some definite thing. (*Crosses slowly to above table. Sheriff crosses down right. Mrs. Hale and Mrs. Peters remain seated at either side of table.*) Something to show—something to make a story about—a thing that would connect up with this strange way of doing it——(*The women's eyes meet for an instant. Enter Hale from outer door.*)

HALE (*remaining by door*): Well, I've got the team around. Pretty cold out there.

COUNTY ATTORNEY: I'm going to stay awhile by myself. (*To the Sheriff.*) You can send Frank out for me, can't you? I want to go over everything. I'm not satisfied that we can't do better.

SHERIFF: Do you want to see what Mrs. Peters is going to take in? (*The Lawyer picks up the apron, laughs.*)

COUNTY ATTORNEY: Oh, I guess they're not very dangerous things the ladies have picked out. (*Moves a few things about, disturbing the quilt pieces which cover the box. Steps back.*) No, Mrs. Peters doesn't need supervising. For that matter a sheriff's wife is married to the law. Ever think of it that way, Mrs. Peters?

MRS. PETERS: Not—just that way.

SHERIFF (*chuckling*): Married to the law. (*Moves to down right door to the other room.*) I just want you to come in here a minute, George. We ought to take a look at these windows.

COUNTY ATTORNEY (*scoffingly*): Oh, windows!

SHERIFF: We'll be right out, Mr. Hale. (*Hale goes outside. The Sheriff follows the County Attorney into the room. Then Mrs. Hale rises, hands tight together, looking intensely at Mrs. Peters, whose eyes make a slow turn, finally meeting Mrs. Hale's. A moment Mrs. Hale holds her, then her own eyes point the way to where the box is concealed. Suddenly Mrs. Peters throws back quilt pieces and tries to put the box in the bag she is carrying. It is too big. She opens box, starts to take bird out, cannot touch it, goes to pieces, stands there helpless. Sound of a knob turning in the other room. Mrs. Hale snatches the box and puts it in the pocket of her big coat. Enter County Attorney and Sheriff, who remains down right.*)

COUNTY ATTORNEY (*crosses to up left door facetiously*): Well, Henry, at least we found out that she was not going to quilt it. She was going to—what is it you call it, ladies?

MRS. HALE (*standing center below table facing front, her hand against her pocket*): We call it—knot it, Mr. Henderson.

[1916]

STUDENT ESSAY: AN ANALYSIS

Sarah Johnson was free to choose the topic and focus of her paper. In the same semester as her literature class, she was enrolled in a philosophy course on ethics where she was introduced to the idea of situational ethics, the notion that exterior pressures often cause people to act in ways they might normally deem unethical, often to prevent or allay a worse evil. This philosophical concept was on Sarah's mind when she read Susan Glaspell's play *Trifles* (pp. 123–134). She noticed that the character of Mrs. Peters does indeed end up behaving in a way she would probably never have imagined for herself. This seemed an interesting concept to pursue, so Sarah decided to trace the development of Mrs. Peters's journey away from her original moral certainty.

Johnson 1

Sarah Johnson

Professor Riley

English 253

24 October 2021

Moral Ambiguity and Character Development
in *Trifles*

What is the relationship between legality and morality? Susan Glaspell's short play *Trifles* asks us to ponder this question, but it provides no clear answers. Part murder mystery, part battle of the sexes, the play makes its readers confront and question many issues about laws, morals, and human relationships. In the person of Mrs. Peters, a sheriff's wife, the play chronicles one woman's moral journey from a certain, unambiguous belief in the law to a more situational view of ethics. Before it is over, this once legally minded woman is even willing to cover up the truth and let someone get away with murder, thus demonstrating that mercy provides its own form of justice in this play.

At the beginning of the play, Mrs. Peters believes that law, truth, and morality are one and the same. Though never unkind,

Sarah focuses on Mrs. Peters right away.

Johnson 2

Mrs. Peters is at first firm in her belief that the men will find the truth and that the crime will be punished as it should be. Mrs. Hale feels the men are "kind of *sneaking*" as they look about Mrs. Wright's abandoned house for evidence against her, but Mrs. Peters assures her that "the law is the law" (129). It is not that Mrs. Peters is less sympathetic toward women than her companion, but she is even more sympathetic toward the lawmen, because her version of morality is so absolute. When the men deride the women's interest in so-called trifles, like sewing and housework, Mrs. Hale takes offense. But Mrs. Peters, convinced that the law must prevail, defends them, saying, "It's no more than their duty," and later, "They've got awful important things on their minds" (127, 129).

Sarah uses direct quotations from the play text as backup for her claims.

As she attempts to comply with the requirements of the law, Mrs. Peters is described in a stage direction as "businesslike," and she tries to maintain a skeptical attitude as she waits for the truth to emerge. Asked if she thinks Mrs. Wright killed her husband, she says, "Oh, I don't know." She seems to be trying to convince herself that the accused is innocent until proven guilty, though she admits that her husband thinks it "looks bad for her." She seems to have absorbed her husband's attitudes and values and to be keeping a sort of legalistic distance from her feelings about the case.

Mrs. Hale is less convinced of the rightness of the men or the law. Even before the two women discover a possible motive for the murder, Mrs. Hale is already tampering with evidence, tearing out the erratic sewing stitches that suggest Mrs. Wright was agitated. Mrs. Peters says, "I don't think we ought to touch things" (129), but she doesn't make any stronger move to stop Mrs. Hale, who continues to fix the sewing. At this point, we see her first beginning to waver from her previously firm stance on right and wrong.

It is not that Mrs. Peters is unsympathetic to the hard life that Mrs. Wright has led. She worries with Mrs. Hale about the accused woman's frozen jars of preserves, her half-done bread, and her unfinished quilt. But she tries to think, like the men, that

Johnson 3

these things are "trifles" and that what matters is the legal truth. But when she sees a bird with a wrung neck, things begin to change in a major way. She remembers the boy who killed her kitten when she was a child, and the sympathy she has felt for Mrs. Wright begins to turn to empathy. The empathy is enough to prompt her first lie to the men. When the county attorney spies the empty birdcage, she corroborates Mrs. Hale's story about a cat getting the bird, even though she knows there was no cat in the house.

In this paragraph, Sarah analyzes a turning point in the play text: a moment in which Mrs. Peters experiences a transformation.

Even after she has reached that point of empathy, Mrs. Peters tries hard to maintain her old way of thinking and of being. Alone again with Mrs. Hale, she says firmly, "We don't know who killed the bird" (132), even though convincing evidence points to John Wright. More important, she says of Wright himself, "We don't know who killed him. We don't *know*" (133). But her repetition and her "rising voice," described in a stage direction, show how agitated she has become. As a believer in the law, she should feel certain that everyone is innocent until proven guilty, but she thinks she knows the truth, and, perhaps for the first time in her life, legal truth does not square with moral truth. Her empathy deepens further still when she thinks about the stillness of the house in which Mrs. Wright was forced to live after the death of her beloved pet, which brought song to an otherwise grim life. She knows Mrs. Wright is childless, and she now remembers not just the death of her childhood kitten but also the terrible quiet in her own house after her first child died. She reaches a moment of crisis between her two ways of thinking when she says, "I know what stillness is. (*Pulling herself back.*) The law has got to punish crimes, Mrs. Hale" (133). This is perhaps the most important line in the chronicle of her growth as a character. First she expresses her newfound empathy with the woman she believes to be a murderer; then, as the stage directions say, she tries to pull herself back and return to the comfortable moral certainty that she felt just a short time before. It is too late for that, though.

Here and elsewhere, Sarah relies on stage directions as evidence for her claims about Mrs. Peters.

In the end, Mrs. Peters gives in to what she believes to be
emotionally right rather than what is legally permissible. She col-
laborates with Mrs. Hale to cover up evidence of the motive and
hide the dead canary. Though very little time has gone by, she
has undergone a major transformation. She may be, as the county
attorney says, "married to the law" (134), but she is also divorced
from her old ideals. When she tries to cover up the evidence, a stage
direction says she "goes to pieces" (134), and Mrs. Hale has to help
her. By the time she pulls herself together, the new woman she is
will be a very different person from the old one. She, along with the
reader, is now in a world where the relationship between legality
and morality is far more complex than she had ever suspected.

Sarah isolates this passage to emphasize the complexity of Mrs. Peters.

Work Cited

Glaspell, Susan. *Trifles. Reading and Writing about Literature:
    A Portable Guide*, edited by Janet E. Gardner and Joanne Diaz,
    5th ed., Bedford/St. Martin's, 2021, pp. 123–34.

CHAPTER 8

Writing a Literary Research Paper

Writing a literary research paper draws on the same set of skills as writing any other paper—choosing a topic, developing a thesis, gathering and organizing support, and so on. The main difference between research writing and other sorts of writing lies in the number and types of sources from which one's support comes. All writing about literature begins with a **primary source**—the poem, story, or play on which the writing is based. Research papers also incorporate **secondary sources**, such as biographical, historical, and critical essays.

As you begin the process of research writing, the most important thing to remember is that you are writing a critical argument. Your paper should not end up reading like a summary of what others have said about the literature. Rather, it should begin and end by making a claim based on your own ideas, and it needs a clear, sharply focused thesis. The sources, both primary and secondary, are there to support your thesis, not to take over the paper.

The method laid out below seems very linear and straightforward: find and evaluate sources for your paper, read them and take notes, and then write a paper integrating material from these sources. In reality, the process is rarely, if ever, this neat. As you read and write, you will discover gaps in your knowledge, or you will ask yourself new questions that will demand more research. Be flexible. Keep in mind that the process of research is recursive, requiring a writer to move back and forth between various stages. Naturally, this means that for research writing, even more than for other kinds of writing, you should start early and give yourself plenty of time to complete the project.

FINDING SOURCES

For many students, research is more or less synonymous with a Google search. It may be easy to think that all the information anybody could ever want is available online and readily and easily accessible to the public. But when it comes to literary research, this is not the case at all. True, there are plenty of websites and newsgroups devoted to literary figures, but the type of information available on these sites tends to be limited to a narrow range—basic biographies of authors, plot summaries, and so forth—and the quality of information is highly variable. Though serious literary scholarship does exist on the website, proprietary online databases (available through a library portal) and print books and journals are still the better sources for you in most cases.

Online Indexes

You can begin to locate sources for your research paper by using the online indexes and databases available through your college or university library. These services sort and index journal and magazine articles to help researchers find what they are looking for. Although using these indexes is somewhat similar to using an internet search engine, the two should not be confused. The internet links to an array of documents—some of very high quality, some worse than useless—that are available for free to the public. By contrast, college, university, and many public libraries pay a fee to allow their users access to the more specialized and highly vetted sources found in various indexes and databases. When you use these services, you are assured that any articles you locate have been published by reliable, respected sources.

Your library probably subscribes to dozens of databases covering many fields of knowledge. These are some of the most useful ones for literary research:

- *Project MUSE* is an acquisition service that provides access to hundreds of scholarly journals in the humanities and social sciences.
- *MLA International Bibliography* (EBSCO) indexes scholarly books and articles on modern languages, literature, folklore, and linguistics; many have full-text links.
- *JSTOR* provides searchable, full-text articles digitized from more than a thousand academic journals, some dating back to the nineteenth century.

These indexes are just a sampling of those most generally applicable to literary research. Depending on your particular topic or interests, you may find yourself drawn to one of the many more specialized indexes, such as *GenderWatch* (for topics related to feminism and other gender issues), *GreenFile* (for environmental topics), and *Hispanic American Periodicals Index*, to name just a few.

If you do not know how to access or use these sources, ask the reference librarian on duty at your college library. Helping students find what they need is this person's principal job, and you will likely learn a lot from him or her. Both your librarian and your instructor can also suggest additional indexes to point you toward good secondary sources. One of the great advantages of databases and indexes is that results can be filtered and sorted according to a wide array of criteria. You can find articles written in a particular year or in a particular language; you can choose to look only at articles that have been peer reviewed (the process that assures scholarly legitimacy); or you can select any of a number of other filters to help you find exactly what you need.

Using the Best Search Terms

When you begin searching, use fairly specific search terms to help the database focus on what you really need and to filter out irrelevant material. Let's say you are researching the nature of love in Shakespeare's sonnets. If you perform a search on the keyword or topic *Shakespeare*, you will get many thousands of hits, many of them about topics unrelated to yours. Searching on both the words *Shakespeare* and *sonnet*, however, will get you closer to what you want, while searching on *Shakespeare*, *sonnet*, and *love* will yield far fewer and far better, more targeted results. If your search nets you fewer results than you expected, try again with different terms (substitute *romance* for *love*, for example). Be patient, and don't be afraid to ask your instructor or librarian for help if you are experiencing difficulty.

Evaluating the Results

Once you have a screen full of results, you will be able to access a **text**, an abstract, or a citation. Some results will give you a link to the complete text of an article; just click on the link, and you can read the article on-screen, print it out, or e-mail it to yourself. Frequently, a link is provided to an abstract, a brief summary (generally just a few sentences) of the content of the full article. Reading an abstract is a good way of finding out whether it is worth tracking down the whole article for your paper. A citation gives only the most basic information about an article — its title, its author, the date of publication, and its page numbers — and it is up to you to then find and read the whole article.

It may be tempting to settle on only those articles available immediately in full-text versions. Don't fall into this trap. Even in this electronic age, scholars and specialists still write books, as well as articles for academic journals that are not always available in electronic versions. Many of the best sources of literary research are available only in print, and the only way to obtain these is to follow the citation's lead and locate the book or journal in the library stacks. If a title or an abstract looks promising, go and retrieve the article. If you think getting up and tracking down a journal is frustrating or time-consuming, imagine how frustrating and time-consuming it will be to attempt to write a research paper without great sources.

Periodicals

At this point, you should be aware of the distinction between two types of periodicals that your search may lead to: magazines, which are directed at a general readership, and scholarly journals, which are written by and for specialists in various academic fields. *Scientific American*, for instance, is a well-respected magazine available on newsstands, whereas *The Journal of Physical Chemistry* is a scholarly journal, generally available only by subscription and read mainly by chemists and chemistry students. In the field of literary studies, there are hundreds of journals, ranging from publications covering a general period or topic (*American Literary Realism*, *Modern Drama*) to those devoted to specific authors (*Walt Whitman Review*, *Melville Society Extracts*).

While magazines like *Time* and *Newsweek* are sometimes appropriate research sources, and you certainly should not rule them out, the most sophisticated literary criticism tends to appear in journals. If you are uncertain whether you are looking at a scholarly journal, look for the following typical characteristics:

- Scholarly journal articles tend to be *longer* than magazine articles, ranging anywhere from five to more than fifty pages.
- Journal articles are *written by specialists* for researchers, professors, and college students. The author's professional credentials and institutional affiliation are often listed.
- Journal articles tend to be written in a given profession's *special language* and can be difficult for nonspecialists to understand. Articles in literary journals use the specialized language of literary theory and criticism.
- Journal articles are usually *peer reviewed* or refereed, meaning that other specialists have read them and determined that they make a significant contribution to the field. Peer referees are often listed as an editorial board on the journal's masthead page.
- Journal articles usually include *footnotes* or *endnotes* and often substantial references, a *bibliography*, or a works cited list.

Books

As mentioned earlier, many scholars still publish their most important work in print books, and the place to look for these is in your college or university library's catalog. (Public libraries, no matter how well run, seldom carry the sorts of specialized sources needed for college-level research.) Start by looking for one or two good books on your topic. Books can be useful at the early stages of your research to help you focus and refine your thinking. If you have given yourself sufficient time for the process, take a book or two home and skim them to determine which parts would be most useful for you. When you return to the library to perform more research, you will have a clearer sense of what you are looking for and therefore will be more efficient at completing the rest of your search. Remember, too, to follow the footnotes: even if a book or article doesn't give you exactly what you need, they might refer you to other authors who have done work that will help you arrive at your thesis.

Interlibrary Loan

If you find a promising lead but discover that your library doesn't have a particular book or has no subscription to the needed periodical, you still may be in luck. Nearly all libraries offer interlibrary loan services, which can track down books and articles from a large network of other libraries and send them to your home institution, generally free of charge. Of course, this process takes time—usually, a couple of days to a couple of weeks—and this is yet another reason to get started as early as possible on your research.

The Internet

Lastly, if your quest for books and periodicals has not yielded all the results you want, remember that the internet can yield some powerful material, if you are strategic in your search. Be sure to ask your instructor or reference librarian about authoritative websites. Your librarian may have already created a special page on the library's website that provides links to the best websites for students of English. If you use the website for your research, look especially for scholarly sites, written by professors or researchers and maintained by colleges and universities. For example, if you want to research the poetry and artwork of William Blake, you might check the William Blake Archive, an online project sponsored by the Library of Congress and the University of North Carolina, Chapel Hill, at www.blakearchive.org/blake/. If you are interested in learning more about Walt Whitman's life and work, check the Walt Whitman Archive, a project developed and edited by Ed Folsom and Kenneth M. Price, both of whom are eminent Whitman scholars, at www.whitmanarchive.org/. If you want to read the 1603 printing of *Hamlet*, check the British Library's website: www.bl.uk/treasures/shakespeare/homepage.html. Also of potential use are the online equivalents of scholarly journals, as well as discussion groups or newsgroups dedicated to particular authors, literary schools, or periods.

How do you know when you have enough sources? Many instructors specify a minimum number of sources for research papers, and many students find exactly that number of sources and then look no further. Your best bet is to stop looking for sources when you think you have enough material to write a top-quality paper. Indeed, it is far better to gather up too many sources and end up not using them all than to get too few and find yourself wanting more information as you write. And remember that any "extra" research beyond what you actually cite in your paper isn't really wasted effort—every piece of information you read contributes to your background knowledge and overall understanding of your topic, making your final paper sound smarter and better informed.

EVALUATING SOURCES

As you locate research sources, you should engage in a continual process of evaluation to determine both the reliability of the potential source and its appropriateness to your particular topic and needs. Keep the following questions in mind to help you evaluate both print and electronic sources:

- **Who is the author, and what are his or her credentials?** Does the author have an academic affiliation? Is the article or book chapter that you've found one of several that the author has written on this subject? Does the author oversee a long-term project on a particular author or historical period? Has the author received grants and fellowships that support his or her work? These are the key questions to ask as you verify the authority of the scholar.
- **What is the medium of publication?** A newspaper article offers factual information and a summary of key points. A magazine article that is several pages long provides more depth than a newspaper article, but it might appeal to a general audience as well. Scholarly journal articles approach a specific problem in a literary work and are usually written for a more specialized audience.

A scholarly book provides a full treatment, and sometimes the scholar addresses a different literary text in each chapter. Books, journals, magazines, newspapers, and electronic publications all have something to offer a researcher, but they do not all offer the same thing. A good researcher will usually seek out a variety of sources.

- **How respectable is the publisher?** Not all publishers are created equal, and some have a much better reputation than others for reliability. Just because something is published, that doesn't make it accurate—think of all of those supermarket tabloids publishing articles about alien autopsies. In general, your best sources are books from university presses and major, well-established publishers; scholarly journal articles; and articles from well-regarded magazines and newspapers such as the *Atlantic Monthly* or the *New York Times*. If you are not sure how respectable or reliable a particular publisher or source might be, ask your instructor or librarian.

- **If it's an online publication, who is hosting the site?** Though commercial sites (whose website addresses end in *.com*) should not be ruled out, keep in mind that these sites are often driven by profit as much as a desire to educate the public. Sites hosted by educational institutions, nonprofit organizations, or the government (*.edu*, *.org*, and *.gov*, respectively) tend to be more purely educational, though they likely won't be free of an agenda, either.

- **How recent is the publication?** While older publications can often be appropriate—you may be doing historical research, or you may want to refer to a classic in a certain field—newer ones are preferable, all other things being equal. Newer publications take advantage of more recent ideas and theories, and they often summarize or incorporate older sources.

- **How appropriate is the source to your specific project?** Even the highest-quality scholarly journal or a book by the top expert in a given field will be appropriate for only a very limited number of research projects. Let your topic, your tentative thesis, and your common sense be your guides.

WORKING WITH SOURCES

You now have a stack of articles and printouts of electronic sources, and perhaps a book or two as well. How do you work through these to get the support you need for your paper?

- *First*, sort the various sources by expected relevance, with those you think will be most informative and useful to you on the top of the list.
- *Next*, skim or read through everything quickly, highlighting or making note of the parts that seem most directly applicable to your paper. (Obviously, you should not mark up or otherwise deface library materials—take notes on a separate piece of paper.)
- *Then*, slow down and reread the important passages again, this time taking careful notes.
- *When taking notes*, keep yourself scrupulously well organized, making sure that you always know which of your notes refers to which source.

If you are taking notes by hand, it's a good idea to start a separate page for each source. If you are using a computer to take notes, start a separate file or section for each new source you read.

Notes will generally fall into one of four categories: quotations, paraphrases, summaries, and commentaries.

Quotations

While quotations are useful, and you will almost certainly incorporate several into your paper, resist the urge to transcribe large portions of text from your sources. Papers that rely too heavily on quotations can be unpleasant reading, with a cluttered or choppy style that results from moving back and forth between your prose and that of the various authors you quote. Reserve direct quoting for those passages that are especially relevant and that you simply can't imagine phrasing as clearly or elegantly yourself. When you do make note of a quotation, be sure to note the pages on which it appears in the source material so that later you will be able to cite it accurately.

Paraphrases and Summaries

Most often, you should take notes in the form of a **paraphrase** or a summary. To paraphrase, simply put an idea or opinion drawn from a source into your own words. Generally, a paraphrase will be about equal in length to the passage being paraphrased, while a summary will be much shorter, capturing the overall point of a passage while leaving out supporting details. Here is a brief passage from *Encyclopædia Britannica Online*'s biography of William Butler Yeats, followed by a paraphrase and a summary:

Normally, Yeats would have been expected to identify with his Protestant tradition — which represented a powerful minority among Ireland's predominantly Roman Catholic population — but he did not. Indeed, he was separated from both historical traditions available to him in Ireland — from the Roman Catholics, because he could not share their faith, and from the Protestants, because he felt repelled by their concern for material success. Yeats's best hope, he felt, was to <u>cultivate</u> a tradition more profound than either the Catholic or the Protestant — the tradition of a hidden Ireland that existed largely in the anthropological evidence of its surviving customs, beliefs, and holy places, more pagan than Christian.

Paraphrase	Summary
Neither Catholicism nor Protestant-ism were useful religious models for Yeats. In Roman Catholicism, he saw a religion that wasn't his, and in Prot-estantism, he saw a religion that was aligned with worldly success. Instead, Yeats looked to the ancient beliefs and customs of pagan Ireland to create meaning in his life and work.	Yeats was more interested in pagan customs of ancient Ireland than in Protestantism or Roman Catholicism.

Paraphrasing and summarizing are usually superior to quoting for two reasons. First, if you can summarize or paraphrase with confidence, then you know you have really understood what you have read. Second, a summary or paraphrase will be more easily transferred from your notes to your paper and will fit in well with your individual prose style. (For more on the use of summary, see pages 52–53.) Just as with quotations, make a note of the page numbers in the source material from which your summaries and paraphrases are drawn.

Commentaries

Finally, some of your notes can be written as commentaries. When something you read strikes you as interesting, you can record your reaction to it. Do you agree or disagree strongly? Why? What exactly is the connection between the source material and your topic or tentative thesis? Making copious commentaries will help you keep your own ideas in the forefront and will keep your paper from devolving into a shopping list of other writers' priorities. Be sure to note carefully when you are commenting rather than summarizing or paraphrasing. When you draft your paper, you will want to distinguish carefully between which ideas are your own and which are borrowed from others.

Keeping Track of Your Sources

As you take notes on the substance of your reading, it is also essential that you record the source's author, title, and publication information for later use in compiling your works cited list, or bibliography. Nothing is more frustrating than having to retrace your research steps on a computer, or even to return to the library, just to get a page reference or the full title of a source. Most accomplished researchers actually put together their works cited list as they go along rather than waiting until the essay is drafted. Such a strategy will ensure that you have all the information you need, and it will save you from the painstaking (and potentially tedious) task of having to create the list all at once at the end of your process.

WRITING THE PAPER

After what may seem like a long time spent gathering and working with your sources, you are now ready to begin the actual writing of your paper.

Refine Your Thesis

Start by looking again at your tentative thesis. Now that you have read a lot and know much more about your topic, does your proposed thesis still seem compelling and appropriate? Do you perhaps need to refine or modify it in order to take into account the information you have learned and opinions you have encountered? If necessary—and it usually is—refine or revise your tentative thesis so that it can help you stay focused as you write. (For advice on what makes a good thesis, see pages 25–29.)

Organize Your Evidence

Just as with any other essay, you will need to organize the evidence in support of your thesis. Follow whatever process for organization you have used successfully in writing other papers, while bearing in mind that this time you will probably have more, and more complex, evidence to deal with. You will likely need an outline—formal or informal—to help you put your materials in a coherent and sensible order. But, once again, flexibility is the key here. As you begin to work your way through the outline, if some different organizational strategy begins to make sense to you, revise your outline rather than forcing your ideas into a preconceived format.

Start Your Draft

The actual drafting of the research paper is probably the part you will find most similar to writing other papers. Try to write fairly quickly and fluently, knowing you can and will add examples, fill in explanations, eliminate redundancies, and work on style during the revision phase. As with your other papers, you may want to write straight through from beginning to end, or you may want to save difficult passages like the introduction for last. Interestingly, many writers find that the process of drafting a research paper actually goes a bit more quickly than does drafting other papers, largely because their considerable research work has left them so well versed in the topic that they have a wealth of ideas for writing.

What might slow you down as you draft your research papers are the citations, which you provide so that a reader knows which ideas are your own and which come from outside sources. Before you begin drafting, familiarize yourself with the conventions for MLA in-text citations (see pages 155–58). Each time you incorporate a quotation, paraphrase, or summary into your essay, you will need to cite the author's name and the relevant page numbers (if available) from the source material. Do not, however, get hung up at this stage trying to remember how to format and punctuate citations. There will be time to hammer out these details later, and it is important as you write to keep your focus on the big picture.

Revise

As you go through the revision process, you should do so with an eye toward full integration of your source material. Are all connections between quotations, paraphrases, or summaries and your thesis clear? Do you include sufficient commentary explaining the inclusion of all source material? Is it absolutely clear which ideas come from which research source? Most important, is the paper still a well-focused argument, meant to convince an audience of the validity of your original thesis? Bearing these questions in mind, you will be ready to make the same sorts of global revision decisions that you would for any other paper—what to add, what to cut, how to reorganize, and so forth. (See pages 34–36 for a reminder of what to look for.)

Edit and Proofread

During the final editing and proofreading stage, include one editorial pass just for checking quotations and documentation format. Make sure each quotation is accurate and exact. Ensure that each reference to a source has an appropriate in-text citation and that your list of works cited (bibliography) is complete and correct. Double-check any manuscript format and punctuation issues you find with the guidelines included in this book or with another appropriate resource. After putting so much time and effort into researching and writing your paper, it would be a shame to have its effectiveness diminished by small inaccuracies or errors.

UNDERSTANDING AND AVOIDING PLAGIARISM

Everyone knows that **plagiarism** is wrong. Buying or borrowing someone else's work, downloading all or part of a paper from the website, and similar practices are beyond reprehensible. Most colleges and universities have codes of academic honesty forbidding such practices and imposing severe penalties—including expulsion from the institution in some cases—on students who are caught breaking them. Many educators feel these penalties are, if anything, not severe enough. Instructors tend to be not only angered but also baffled by students who plagiarize. In addition to the obvious wrongs of cheating and lying (nobody likes being lied to), students who plagiarize are losing out on a learning opportunity, a waste of the student's, and instructor's, time.

Not everyone, though, is altogether clear on what plagiarism entails, and a good deal of plagiarism can actually be unintentional on the part of the student. A working definition of *plagiarism* will help to clarify what plagiarism is:

- presenting someone else's ideas as your own
- using information from any print or electronic source without fully citing the source
- buying or "borrowing" a paper from any source
- submitting work that someone else has written, in whole or in part
- having your work edited to the point that it is no longer your work
- submitting the same paper for more than one class without the express permission of the instructors involved

Some of this is obvious. You know it is cheating to have a friend do your homework or to download a paper from the website and submit it as your own. But the first and last items on the list are not as clear-cut or self-explanatory. What exactly does it mean to present someone else's ideas as your own? Many students believe that as long as they rephrase an idea into their own words, they have done their part to avoid plagiarism; however, they are mistaken. Readers reasonably assume that everything in your paper is a product of your own thinking, not just your own phrasing, unless you share credit with another by documenting your source. No matter how it is phrased, an original idea belongs to the person who first thought of it and wrote it down; in fact, the notion of possession in this context is so strong that the term applied to such ownership is *intellectual property*.

As an analogy, imagine you have invented a revolutionary product, patented it, and put it up for sale. The next week, you find that your neighbor has produced the same product, painted it a different color, changed the name, and is doing a booming business selling the product. Is your neighbor any less guilty of stealing your idea just because he or she is using a new name and color for the product? Of course not. Your intellectual property, the idea behind the product, has been stolen. And you are no less guilty of plagiarism if you glean a piece of information, an opinion, or even an abstract concept from another person, put it into your own words, and "sell" it in your paper without giving proper credit.

Let us say, for example, that you find this passage about William Butler Yeats:

> Religious by temperament but unable to accept orthodox Christianity, Yeats throughout his life explored esoteric philosophies in search of a tradition that would substitute for a lost religion. He became a member of the Theosophical Society and the Order of the Golden Dawn, two groups interested in Eastern occultism, and later developed a private system of symbols and mystical ideas.

Drawing from this passage this chart provides an example of plagiarism as well as how to avoid it:

Plagiarism	Appropriate Use of a Source
Religious throughout his life, Yeats explored a wide variety of faith practices. He became a member of the Theosophical Society and the Order of the Golden Dawn, two groups interested in Eastern occultism. Later, he developed his own private religious system.	Yeats rejected the Christianity of his native Ireland, but he became interested in occultism and Eastern philosophy. From these sources, he developed his own system of mystical symbols that he used in his poetry.

The example of plagiarism in the left column relies too heavily on the original text, whereas the prose in the right column uses elements of the original and adds other information as well. However, the essential line of reasoning and the central point of both passages are largely the same. If your prose too closely resembles the prose of the author or critic and you do not acknowledge the original source, *this is plagiarism*.

Finally, let's look at the last item on the list: submitting the same paper for more than one class without the express permission of the instructors involved. Sometimes, you will find substantial overlap in the subject matter of two or more of your classes. A literature class, for instance, has elements of history, psychology, sociology, and other disciplines, and once in a while you might find yourself working on writing projects in courses that share common features. You might be tempted to let your research and writing in such a case do double duty, and there is not necessarily anything wrong with that. However, if you wish to write a paper on a single topic for more than one class, clear these plans with both instructors first. And, of course, even if you use the same research sources for both assignments, you will almost certainly need to write two separate essays, tailoring each to meet the specifications of individual classes and disciplines.

WHAT TO DOCUMENT AND WHAT *NOT* TO DOCUMENT

Everything borrowed from another source needs to be documented. Obviously, you should document every direct quotation of any length from primary or secondary sources. Equally important is the documentation of all your paraphrases and summaries of ideas, information, and opinions, citing authors and page numbers. The rule of thumb is that if you didn't make it up yourself, you should probably document it.

The word *probably* in the previous sentence suggests that there are exceptions, and indeed there are. You do not need to document proverbial sayings ("Live and let live.") or very familiar quotations ("I have a dream . . ."), though in the case of the latter you may want to allude to the speaker in your text. You also do not need to document any information that can be considered common knowledge. Common knowledge here refers not only to information that you would expect nearly every adult to know immediately (that Shakespeare wrote *Hamlet*, for instance, or that George Washington was the first president of the United States). Common knowledge also encompasses undisputed information that you could look up in a general or specialized reference work. The average person on the street probably couldn't tell you that T. S. Eliot was born in 1888, but you don't need to say where that piece of information comes from, as it is widely available to anyone who wishes to find it.

Use both your common sense and your sense of fairness to make any necessary decisions about whether or not to document something. When in doubt, ask your instructor, and remember, it's better to document something unnecessarily than to be guilty of plagiarism.

DOCUMENTING SOURCES: MLA FORMAT

This section includes information on how to document the following:

Some students seem to believe that English teachers find footnotes and bibliographies and textual citations fun and interesting. In truth, few people know better than those who have to teach it how tedious format and documentation can be for a writer. Chances are your instructor will insist that you document your sources. There are at least three reasons for requiring documentation. First, a sense of fair play demands that we give proper credit to those whose ideas benefit us. Second, by documenting your sources, you make it possible for your readers to find the sources themselves and follow up if they become interested in something in your paper. Third, documenting your sources, and doing it accurately, enhances your credibility as a writer by highlighting your professionalism and thoroughness.

There are many different forms and formulas for documenting sources—the APA (American Psychological Association) format commonly used in the social sciences, the CBE (Council of Biology Editors) format used in the life sciences, the *Chicago* (*Chicago Manual of Style*) format used in history, and so on. Each system highlights the type of information most relevant to experts in a particular field. If you have received contradictory instructions about documentation format for research projects in the past—include dates in your in-text references or don't; use footnotes or use endnotes—chances are you were working in different documentation systems. The format most often used in the humanities is MLA, the system developed by the Modern Language Association.

MLA format is comprised of two main elements: in-text citations and a works cited list (*bibliography*). In-text citations are parenthetical references that follow each quotation, paraphrase, or summary and give the briefest possible information about the source, usually the author's last name and a page number. The works cited list, which comes at the end of the paper, gives more detailed information about all sources used. The idea is that a reader coming across a parenthetical reference in your text can easily turn to the works cited list and get full details about the type of publication from which the material comes, the date of publication, and so on. (Some writers use a third element of MLA style, content endnotes, which come between the end of the paper and the works cited list and contain extra information not readily integrated into the paper. Although you may use endnotes if you wish, they are not necessary.)

The following pages describe the major types of sources you are likely to encounter and how to reference those sources both in the text of your research paper and in your works cited list. The information here, however, is not exhaustive. If you want to cite a source not covered here, or if you would like more information about MLA style and citation format, turn to the following book:

MLA Handbook, 8th edition. Modern Language Association, 2016.

In-Text Citations

The purpose of an in-text citation is to give a very brief acknowledgment of a source within the body of your essay. In MLA format, in-text citations take the form of brief parenthetical interruptions directly following each quotation, paraphrase, or summary. Some students find these interruptions a bit distracting at first, but you will quickly find that you grow accustomed to them and that soon they will not slow your reading or comprehension. The following explanations and examples of in-text citations should cover most instances you will encounter.

Citing Author and Page Number in Parentheses

Typically, a citation will contain the last name of the author being cited and a page number. The first example here shows a direct quotation, the second a paraphrase.

One reviewer referred to *Top Girls* as, "among other things, a critique of bourgeois feminism" (Munk 33).

When English wool was in demand, the fens were rich, but for many years now they have been among the poorest regions in England (Chamberlain 13).

Coming across these references in your text, your readers will know that they can turn to your works cited list and find out the full names of Munk and Chamberlain, the titles of what they have written, and where, when, and in what medium the works were published.

Citing the Author in Body Text and Only the Page Number in Parentheses

If you have already named the author in your own text, for instance in a lead-in phrase, you do not need to repeat the name in parentheses, as your reader will already know which author to look for in your works cited list. In this case, the parenthetical reference need only contain the page number. The two examples already given could be rewritten as follows:

Reviewer Erika Munk referred to *Top Girls* as, "among other things, a critique of bourgeois feminism" (33).

Martha Chamberlain writes that when English wool was in demand, the fens were rich, but for many years now they have been among the poorest regions in England (13).

Citing Multiple Pages in a Source

You may find yourself wanting to make a brief summary of an extended passage, in which case you might need to cite the inclusive pages of the summarized material.

John McGrath's Scottish theater company was destroyed by the end of government subsidies, as Elizabeth MacLennan chronicles in *The Moon Belongs to Everyone* (137–99).

Citing a Source without Page Numbers

Many electronic publications do not have page numbers. If you are citing one of these sources, simply give the author's last name either in parentheses or in a signal phrase before the quotation or summary.

> Critics have noted that "Dickinson declined to make the public confession of faith that would admit her to the church" (Yezzi).

or

> David Yezzi writes that "Dickinson declined to make the public confession of faith that would admit her to the church."

Citing Multiple Sources at Once

Sometimes several different sources say roughly the same thing, or at least there is substantial overlap in the parts you want to cite. Following are two ways of handling this situation; use whichever one best suits your needs.

> This particular passage in the play has been the source of much critical speculation, especially by Freudian critics (Anders 19; Olsen 116; Smith 83–84; Watson 412).

> A number of Freudian critics have commented on this passage, including Anders (19), Olsen (116), Smith (83–84), and Watson (412).

Citing Two or More Sources by the Same Author

It is common for one author to write multiple books or articles on the same general topic, and you might want to use more than one of them in your paper. In this case, a shortened version of the title must appear in the parenthetical reference, to show which work by the author is being quoted or cited. In the citations for an article and a book about playwright Caryl Churchill, both by the author Geraldine Cousin, one would give the first word of the work's title (other than *the*, *a*, and so forth). As seen below, *Common* and *Churchill* are the first words in the title of the article and the book, respectively:

> Churchill claims that this sentiment was expressed to her by one of the gangmasters she encountered in the fens (Cousin, "Common" 6).

> Churchill's notebooks from her visit to the fens record her seeing baby prams parked around the fields in which the women worked (Cousin, *Churchill* 47).

Note the comma between the author's name and the title. Note that these shortened titles are formatted (with italics or quotation marks) just as they would be in the works cited list or elsewhere in your writing, in quotation marks for an article and in italics (or underscored) for a book.

If the author is named in a signal phrase, only the shortened title and page number are needed in the parenthetical reference.

"Violence," says Ruby Cohn, "is the only recourse in these brutalized lives on the Fen" (*Retreats* 139).

Citing a Quotation or Source within a Source

On page 58 of his book about Margaret Thatcher, Charles Moser writes:

In a speech to Parliament in June of 1983, Thatcher said, "A return to Victorian values will encourage personal responsibility, personal initiative, self-respect, and respect for others and their property."

Let us say you do not have the text of Thatcher's original speech and that Moser doesn't make reference to a primary source that you can track down. But Moser is a reliable author, so you believe the Thatcher quotation is accurate and want to use a portion of it in your paper. This is done by giving the original speaker's name (in this case Margaret Thatcher) in your text and using the abbreviation *qtd. in* and the author from whom you got the quote (in this case Charles Moser) in the parenthetical citation.

These "Victorian values," Thatcher claimed, would "encourage personal responsibility, personal initiative, self-respect, and respect for others" (qtd. in Moser 58).

Preparing Your Works Cited List

It is a good idea to begin preparing your works cited list during the research process, adding new entries each time you find a source that might be useful to you. That way, when the time comes to finalize your paper, you can just edit the list you already have, making sure it contains all the necessary entries and no extraneous ones, and checking each for accuracy and format. If you wait until the end to create your works cited list, you will have to compile the whole list from scratch at a time when you are most tired and therefore least able to focus your attention on this necessary, detailed work.

A number of online resources exist to help you compose and format your works cited. Two of the best respected are *easybib.com* and *citationmachine.net*. These sites allow you to select the type of source from a menu and then enter information about author names, titles, and so on in a form. Once all the information is entered, the software formats and punctuates it appropriately, and you can then save it to your document. You can choose from MLA, APA, or other popular formats. Most instructors do not mind you using these services (ask if you are unsure how your instructor feels about this), but a word of caution is needed. These services can format and punctuate, but they cannot proofread. They will use the information exactly as you enter it, so you must double-check for accuracy before submitting the information for formatting. Many word-processing programs also have bibliography generators, but these are usually not adequate for specialized, scholarly sources and are therefore not recommended.

General Guidelines

- **Begin your list of works cited on a new page.** Continue paginating as you have throughout the paper, with your last name and the page number appearing in the upper right corner.
- **Center the heading Works Cited at the top of the page** in capital and lowercase letters; do not use italics, boldface print, or quotation marks.
- **Arrange the sources alphabetically, by the last name of the source's author** (or by title, in the case of anonymous works), regardless of the order in which the sources are cited in your paper.
- **Begin each entry flush with the left margin.** When an entry takes up more than one line, all lines after the first are indented a half an inch. (For an example, see the works cited list in the research paper by Rachel McCarthy, on page 172.) This is called a *hanging indent*, and all major word-processing programs can be set to format your entries this way.
- **Double-space the entire list.**
- **Do not put extra line spaces between entries.**
- **As always, carefully follow any additional or contrary instructions provided by your instructor.**

Citing Books

To list books in your works cited, include as much of the following information as is available and appropriate, in the following order and format. Each works cited entry has three basic parts, or containers:

Author's Name. *Title of Work*. Publication Information.

Copy your entries directly from the book's title page, which provides more complete and accurate information than does a cover or another bibliography. The following examples cover most of the sorts of books you are likely to encounter.

A book by a single author.   The simplest entry is a single-volume book by a single author, not part of a series, and without additional editors, translators, or compilers.

> Alexie, Sherman. *The Absolutely True Diary of a Part-Time Indian*. Little,
> Brown, 2007.

If a book has an editor, a translator, or a compiler in addition to an author, identify this person by role and by name, between the book's title and publisher.

> Sebald, W. G. *The Rings of Saturn*. Translated by Michael Hulse, New
> Directions, 1998.

The following example cites a third-edition book by a single author.

> Richter, David H. *The Critical Tradition: Classic Texts and Contemporary Trends*.
> 3rd ed., Bedford/St. Martin's, 2007.

A book by two authors.   Note that in the following example only the first author's name appears in reverse order. UP (with no periods) is the abbreviation for University Press. Note also the series title, Oxford Shakespeare Topics, is included when citing a book in a series.

> Gurr, Andrew, and Mariko Ichikawa. *Staging in Shakespeare's Theaters*. Oxford
> UP, 2000. Oxford Shakespeare Topics.

A book by three or more authors.   If three or more authors or editors are listed on a book's title page, you can list all names or give only the name of the first, followed by *et al.* (Latin for "and others").

> Gardner, Janet E., et al., editors. *Literature: A Portable Anthology*. 5th ed.,
> Bedford/St. Martin's, 2021.

A book by an unknown or anonymous author.   Simply include all the other information, beginning with the title.

> *Gilgamesh: A New English Version*. Translated by Stephen Mitchell, Free, 2006.

A book by a corporate author.   Corporate authorship refers to a book that lists an organization rather than an individual as its author. This is especially common with publications from government and nonprofit organizations.

> Bureau of the Census. *Historical Statistics of the United States, 1789–1945: A Supplement to the Statistical Abstract of the United States*. Government Printing Office, 1945.

Two or more books by the same author.   If you cite more than one work by a single author, alphabetize the entries by title. For the second and all subsequent entries by the same author, replace the author's name with three hyphens.

> Bloom, Harold. *Hamlet: Poem Unlimited*. Riverhead-Penguin, 2003.

> ---. *Shakespeare's Poems and Sonnets*. Chelsea, 1999. Bloom's Major Poets.

A work in an anthology or compilation.   The first example that follows is a citation from a literature anthology; the second is from a scholarly work in which each chapter is written by a different author. The title of the work or chapter being cited is usually enclosed in quotation marks. However, if the piece is a play or novel, you should italicize its title instead.

> Baldwin, James. "Sonny's Blues." *Literature: A Portable Anthology*, edited by Janet E. Gardner et al., 5th ed., Bedford/St. Martin's, 2021, pp. 358–84.

> Keyishian, Harry. "Shakespeare and the Movie Genre: The Case of *Hamlet*." *The Cambridge Companion to Shakespeare on Film*, edited by Russell Jackson, Cambridge UP, 2000, pp. 72–81.

Two or more works in a single anthology or compilation.   If you cite two or more works from a single anthology or collection, you can create a cross-reference, citing the full publication information for the collection as a whole and cross-referencing the individual pieces using only the name of the editor and page numbers of the particular work within the anthology or compilation.

> Chopin, Kate. "The Story of an Hour." Gardner and Diaz, pp. 99–101.

> Gardner, Janet E., and Joanne Diaz, editors. *Reading and Writing about Literature: A Portable Guide*. 5th ed., Bedford/St. Martin's, 2021.

> Gilman, Charlotte Perkins. "The Yellow Wallpaper." Gardner and Diaz, pp. 85–99.

An article in a reference work.   The format for citing material from dictionaries, encyclopedias, or other specialized reference works is similar to that for a work in an anthology, but the name of the reference work's editor is omitted. Often, such reference articles are anonymous anyway. The first example is for a signed article in a print book, the second for an anonymous entry in an electronic encyclopedia.

> Brown, Andrew. "Sophocles." *The Cambridge Guide to Theatre*. Cambridge UP,
> 1988, pp. 899–900.

> Durante, Amy M. "Finn Mac Cumhail." *Encyclopedia Mythica*, 17 Apr. 2011,
> www.pantheon.org/articles/f/finn_mac_cumhail.html.

An introduction, preface, foreword, or afterword.   After the author's name, give the name of the part of the book being cited, capitalized but neither italicized nor in quotation marks, followed by the title of the book and all relevant publication information.

> Dunham, Lena. Foreword. *The Liars' Club*, by Mary Karr, Penguin Classics,
> 2015, pp. xi–xiii.

Citing Periodicals

An article in a scholarly journal.   Most scholarly journals publish several issues in each annual volume and paginate continuously throughout the entire volume. (In other words, if one issue ends on page 230, the next will begin with page 231.) Your works cited entry should list the author, article title, journal title, volume number, issue number, the season or month and year and page numbers. Follow the punctuation shown here exactly.

> Fuqua, Amy. " 'The Furrow of His Brow': Providence and Pragmatism in
> Toni Morrison's *Paradise*." *Midwest Quarterly*, vol. 54, no. 1, Autumn
> 2012, pp. 38–52.

An article in a magazine.   For an article in a magazine, omit the volume and issue numbers (if given) and include the date of publication. The first example here shows the format for a monthly, bimonthly, or quarterly magazine; the second, which includes the date as well as the month, is appropriate for weekly and biweekly magazines.

> Bryan, Christy. "Ivory Worship." *National Geographic*, Oct. 2012, pp. 28–61.

> Grossman, Lev. "A Star Is Born." *Time*, 2 Nov. 2015, pp. 30–39.

An article in a newspaper.   When a newspaper is separated into sections, note the letter or number designating the section as a part of the page reference. Newspapers and some magazines frequently place articles on nonconsecutive pages. When this happens, give the number of the first page only, followed by the plus sign (+).

> Sherry, Allison. "Volunteers' Personal Touch Turns High-Tech Data into
>
> Votes." *The Denver Post*, 30 Oct. 2012, pp. 1A+.

A review.   To cite a review, you must include the title and author of the work being reviewed between the review title and the periodical title. The first entry that follows is for a book review in a newspaper. The second is a review of a film in a magazine that includes the director's name.

> Walton, James. "Noble, Embattled Souls." Review of *The Bone Clocks*
>
> and *Slade House*, by David Mitchell, *The New York Review of Books*,
>
> 3 Dec. 2015, pp. 55–58.

> Lane, Anthony. "Film within a Film." Review of *Argo*, directed by Ben Affleck,
>
> and *Sinister*, directed by Scott Derrickson, *The New Yorker*, 15 Oct. 2012,
>
> pp. 98–99.

Citing Electronic Sources

Sometimes online sources do not list all the information required for a complete citation. They are, for instance, frequently anonymous, and they do not always record the dates when they were written or updated. Give as much of the information as you can find, using the formats that follow. Whenever possible, include permalinks (also known as Digital Object Identifiers, or DOIs) in place of URLs. Note that the date the researcher accessed the document is optional. Include it for online sources that do not have a publication date.

An article from an online subscription database or index.   When you access an article through an online index or database (*MLA International Bibliography*, *JSTOR*, etc.), treat it as you would a print source, with the addition of the title of the database (italicized), and the permalink or URL.

> Bottomore, Stephen. "The Romance of the Cinematograph." *Film*
>
> *History*, vol. 24, no. 3, July 2012, pp. 341–44. *JSTOR*, doi:10.2979
>
> /filmhistory.24.3.341.

An online scholarly project or database.   A full entry for an online scholarly project or database includes the editor's name; the title of the project, italicized; the name of the sponsoring organization or institution; the date of the project's most recent update; and the permalink or URL.

> Folsom, Ed, and Kenneth M. Price, editors. *The Walt Whitman Archive*. Walt
> Whitman Archive, April 2016, whitmanarchive.org.

An online journal or magazine.   The first entry that follows is from an online scholarly journal; the second entry is from an online popular magazine.

> Bryson, Devin. "The Rise of a New Senegalese Cultural Philosophy?" *African*
> *Studies Quarterly*, vol. 14, no. 3, Mar. 2014, pp. 33–56, asq.africa.ufl
> .edu/files/Volume-14-Issue-3-Bryson.pdf.

> Leonard, Andrew. "The Surveillance State High School." *Salon*, 27 Nov. 2012,
> www.salon.com/2012/11/27/the_surveillance_state_high_school/.

A professional or personal website.   Include as much of the following information as appropriate and available: the author of the document or site; the document title, in quotation marks (if the site is divided into separate documents); the name of the site, italicized; the sponsoring organization or institution; the date of creation or most recent update; and the permalink or URL. If the site has no official title, provide a brief identifying phrase, neither italicized nor in quotation marks, as in the second example below.

> Railton, Stephen. *Mark Twain in His Times*. Stephen Railton / U of Virginia
> Library, 2012, twain.lib.virginia.edu/.

> Bae, Rebecca. Home page. Iowa State U, 2015, www.engl.iastate.edu/rebecca
> -bae-directory-page/.

Short work from a website.   For an individual page on a website, list the author (if given), followed by the rest of the information for the entire website, as above.

> Enzinna, Wes. "Syria's Unknown Revolution." *Pulitzer Center on Crisis*
> *Reporting*, 24 Nov. 2015, pulitzercenter.org/projects/middle-east
> -syria-enzinna-war-rojava.

A blog post.   An entry for a blog citation includes the blogger's name (or online handle), the title of the posting, the blog title, the date of posting, and the permalink or the URL.

Cimons, Marlene. "Why Cities Could Be the Key to Solving the Climate
Crisis." *Thinkprogress.org*, Center for American Progress Action Fund,
10 Dec. 2015, thinkprogress.org/climate/2015/12/10/3730938/cities
-key-to-climate-crisis/.

A Facebook post or comment.

Bedford English. "Stacey Cochran explores Reflective Writing in the
classroom and as a writer: ow.ly/YkjVB." *Facebook*, 15 Feb. 2016,
www.facebook.com/BedfordEnglish/posts/10153415001259607.

A Twitter post (tweet).

Curiosity Rover. "Can you see me waving? How to spot #Mars in the night
sky: youtu.be/hv8hVvJlcJQ." *Twitter*, 5 Nov. 2015, 11:00 a.m., twitter
.com/marscuriosity/status/672859022911889408.

A posting to a discussion list or newsgroup.   Give the author's name,
the title of the posting (in quotation marks) taken from the subject line,
the title of the site on which the forum is found (italicized), the sponsor
of the site, the date of posting, and the permalink or URL. If the posting
has no title, use the identifying phrase *online posting*.

Robin, Griffith. "Write for the Reading Teacher." *Developing Digital Literacies*,
NCTE, 23 Oct. 2015, ncte.connectedcommunity.org/communities
/community-home/digestviewer/viewthread?GroupId=1693&MID
=24520&tab=digestviewer&CommunityKey=628d2ad6-8277-4042
-a376-2b370ddceabf.

Citing Other Miscellaneous Sources

A television or radio program.   Begin with the name of the author or
another individual (director, narrator, and so forth), only if you refer primarily to the work of a particular individual. Otherwise, begin with the
title of a segment or episode (if appropriate), in quotation marks; the
title of the program, italicized; the title of the series (if applicable), italicized; the name of the network; and the date of broadcast.

"Free Speech on College Campuses." *Washington Journal*, narrated by
Peter Slen, C-SPAN, 27 Nov. 2015.

The Daily Show with Trevor Noah. Comedy Central, 18 Nov. 2015.

A film.   Film citations begin with the film title, which is italicized, followed by the name of the director, the names of the featured key performers, the name of the movie studio, and the year of release.

> *Birdman or (The Unexpected Virtue of Ignorance).* Directed by Alejandro
>   González Iñárritu, performances by Michael Keaton, Emma Stone, Zach
>   Galifianakis, Edward Norton, and Naomi Watts, Fox Searchlight, 2014.

An interview.   Begin with the name of the person interviewed. For a published interview, give the title, if any, in quotation marks (if there is no title, simply use the designation *Interview*, neither in quotation marks nor italicized), followed by the name of the interviewer, and publication information. The first example that follows is for an interview published in a magazine. The second example is for an interview conducted personally by the author of the research paper and gives the name of the person interviewed.

> Weddington, Sarah. "Sarah Weddington: Still Arguing for *Roe.*" Interview by
>   Michele Kort, *Ms.*, Winter 2013, pp. 32–35.

> Akufo, Dautey. Personal interview, 11 Apr. 2016.

A lecture or speech.   To cite a speech or lecture that you've attended, use the following format, listing the speaker's name; the title of the presentation, in quotation marks (if announced or published); the sponsoring organization; the location; the date; and a descriptive label such as *Address* or *Lecture*.

> Smith, Anna Deavere. "On the Road: A Search for American Character."
>   National Endowment for the Humanities, John F. Kennedy Center for the
>   Performing Arts, Washington, 6 Apr. 2015. Address.

Generally speaking, you do not need to cite a class lecture; to quote or otherwise refer to something an instructor says in class, you may do so simply by crediting the instructor in the text of your essay.

A letter or e-mail.   There are three kinds of letters: published, unpublished (in archives), and personal. A published letter includes the writer's name, the recipient's name (in quotation marks), the date of the letter, the number of the letter (if assigned by the editor), and publication information for the book or periodical in which it appears.

> Wharton, Edith. Letter to Henry James, 28 Feb. 1915. *Henry James and Edith
>   Wharton: Letters, 1900–1915*, edited by Lyall H. Powers, Scribner, 1990,
>   pp. 323–26.

In citing an unpublished letter, give the writer's name, the title or a description of the material (for example, *Letter to Havelock Ellis*), the date, and any identifying number assigned to it. Include the name of the library or institution housing the material.

> Sanger, Margaret. Letter to Havelock Ellis. 14 July 1924. Margaret Sanger
>   Papers, Sophia Smith Collection, Smith College.

To cite a letter you received personally, include the author, the designation "Letter to [author's name should go here]," and the date posted. To cite an e-mail you received personally, include the author, the subject line as the title, who the message was received by, and the date it was sent.

> Green, Barclay. Letter to the author. 1 Sept. 2015.

> Thornbrugh, Caitlin. "Coates Lecture." Received by Rita Anderson,
>   20 Oct. 2015.

A work of visual art.   Give the artist's name, the title of the artwork (in italics), the date of composition, the medium of composition, and, if you saw the original artwork in person, the name and location of the institution that houses the artwork. If you saw the artwork online, be sure to provide the permalink or the URL.

> Goya, Francisco. *The Family of Charles IV*. 1800. Oil on canvas. Museo del
>   Prado, Madrid.

> Clough, Charles. *January Twenty-First*. 1988–89, Joslyn Art Museum, Omaha,
>   www.joslyn.org/collections-and-exhibitions/permanent-collections
>   /modern-and-contemporary/charles-clough-january-twenty-first/.

STUDENT ESSAY: SAMPLE RESEARCH PAPER

When choosing a research paper topic, Rachel McCarthy recalled how interesting she had found Yeats's poem "The Second Coming" (p. 11), which used such visceral imagery of—and allusions to—the Apocalypse. Rachel decided to see what professional literary critics had to say on the subject and how closely their ideas matched her own. Her paper, which follows, combines a close reading of the primary literary text with research from secondary sources.

Rachel McCarthy

Professor Diaz

English 204

2 April 2021

The Widening Gyres of Chaos in Yeats's

"The Second Coming"

Although unknown to astronomers in 1919 when William Butler Yeats wrote "The Second Coming," we live in an ever-expanding universe, which, much like Yeats's "widening gyre" (line 1), is predicted to keep expanding until the eventual heat death of the cosmos. However, when Yeats wrote his great poem, he had already developed a theory of historical epochs that took the shape of gyres. In the pages of his journal, he envisioned two interlocking cones representing opposing traits—facts vs. emotions, art vs. morals, subjectivity vs. objectivity, and so on—with different traits being valued more than the other at various points in history (Unterecker 25). Paul D. Deane, a researcher in vocabulary and linguistics, argues that Yeats's use of this cyclical imagery underscores the new, inverted world order that is ushered in by the "rough beast." Even so, the poem takes place in a *widening* gyre, which suggests an alarming departure from the normal movement between different stages of Yeats's gyre. Paul Deane suggests that Yeats's "widening gyre" is a metaphor for historical change that reveals an underlying unity in the poem; however, I would argue that in "The Second Coming," Yeats uses imagery of disunity and chaos in order to create a feeling of horror of "The Second Coming," thus exploiting readers' fears of the unknown.

Rachel focuses on one Yeats poem.

Rachel demonstrates how she is in conversation with a scholar, and then she builds upon that conversation to create a contestable thesis statement.

From the start, the poem builds tension by establishing a sense of helplessness and uncertainty. The falcon is no longer within earshot of the falconer who is supposed to control the bird; and the gyre of history widens until "mere anarchy is loosed upon the world" (Yeats 4). The poem lacks a unifying meter or rhyme scheme to orient readers; and as for setting, we only know that the "ceremony of innocence" is being drowned "everywhere" (6),

Here and elsewhere, Rachel uses direct quotations from Yeats's poem in order to substantiate her claims.

McCarthy 2

while a monster lurks "somewhere in the sands of the desert" with a "gaze blank and pitiless as the sun" (13, 15). Deane observes that this monster's "physical center, its torso, is that of a lion, not a man," and consequently "lacks both a heart and soul" (639–40), hence its inability to feel pity for humankind. I would argue that this absence of a central identity adds to the sphinx being a symbol of mystery, as sphinxes from Greek mythology are famous for posing riddles to their victims before devouring them.

Yet despite the terrifying presence of the monster, the poem does not suggest that the monster is to blame for the Apocalypse; disaster just inexplicably *happens*. The repetition of the passive phrase "is loosed" (5–6) in the first stanza reinforces this idea that things have spiraled completely out of control, without any apparent agent of action. The second stanza's insistence that "surely the Second Coming is at hand" (10) should mark a turning point in this chaos, like a volta in a sonnet, when heavenly forces arrive to put an end to the horrific reality of the first stanza. When the beast awakens instead, this only adds to the mounting anxiety. Whereas the poem begins with definitive assertions that "things [are falling] apart" and "the centre cannot hold" (4), it ends with a question that fails to resolve the narrative tension: "What rough beast, its hour come round at last,/Slouches towards Bethlehem to be born?" (21–22). With looming disaster being the only certainty in a poem titled "The Second Coming," we can no longer be certain if Christ is indeed coming at all.

Our framework for understanding the world relies on cycles — war and peace, birth and death, the Earth's orbit around the sun — which Yeats leverages in order to create a distorted version of the New Testament for the Antichrist. Deane notes multiple uses of circular imagery, from the falcon blindly circling the falconer to the desert birds that circle over the beast, signifying how a world once centered around Christianity is re-centering itself around a creature with "no moral balance," who can only "increase the moral imbalance of the periphery" (640). The focus on cyclical

Rachel provides a smooth transition between one idea and the next.

Here, Rachel relies upon her research in the dictionary and the Bible in order to deepen the complexity of her analysis.

motion makes sense, given that the Second Coming promises a cycle, that just as Christ was here two thousand years ago, so too will he come again. And here, history is repeating itself, but with a darker twist. In the "ceremony of innocence," the Catholic sacrament of Baptism, holy water is replaced with a tide of blood; similarly, the desert, a place of spiritual purity from which John the Baptist emerged to announce the coming of the Messiah, is remade into the dominion of world-ending monsters. "Darkness drops again" (18), the speaker adds, alluding to how darkness fell over Jerusalem when Jesus was crucified (*New Oxford Annotated Bible*, Matt. 27.45). And most overtly, the beast is preparing to be born in Bethlehem in Christ's place. In short, the beast subverts our expectations by twisting familiar images and ideas into something nightmarish. *Apokalypsis* is the Greek word for "revelation" ("apocalypse, noun"), giving a double meaning to the second stanza's plea that "surely some revelation is at hand; / Surely the Second Coming is at hand" (9–10). Much to our horror, deliverance from evil and that evil itself seem to be intertwined because of the beast.

What makes the beast horrifying is its ability to break apart the cycles upon which our orderly world depends, creating a new era of uncertainty and fear by the poem's end. Deane interprets this ending as "the rough beast slouching in from the desert, from the edge of things, to the very center, to be born as Christ was, replacing the willing obedience of Christian society with its own horrific social and moral order" (640). However, this conclusion that the beast has become the new center of human existence ignores the fact that human existence as we understand it is coming to an end. The old order of things has come to an end, yes, signaled by the fact that the beast's "hour [has] come round at last" (19), but the beast does little to carve out a new one. Instead, it ominously "slouches towards Bethlehem" (20). For the first time in a poem of turning gyres and circling desert birds, we are instead given a creature moving purposefully in a single direction.

Again, Rachel shows that she is in conversation with a scholar and demonstrates how her reading differs from his.

McCarthy 4

Here, the natural order of time also breaks down, as the beast paradoxically prepares itself to be born, and we no longer know what to expect once it arrives at Bethlehem. Compared with the beast in Revelation, which rises "out of the sea with ten horns and seven heads" crowned with horns and blasphemous words, and possesses "feet like a bear's" and "the mouth of a lion" (*New Oxford Annotated Bible,* Rev. 13.1–3), Yeats's "rough beast" seems purposefully unimaginative, yet its ambiguity adds to its horror, as it exists beyond our limited imaginations. Just as the gyre is widening beyond its natural limits, so too is the beast subverting our expectations in order to create a new future which is dark and unknowable.

The purpose of the Book of Revelation was to bring hope to a group of people faced with an uncertain future due to religious persecution under the Roman Empire, but reassurance does not seem to be Yeats's aim. Instead, he intentionally disorients us as he leaves more questions than answers. His bleak vision of the future does not even appear to come with a warning, for it seems that nothing can be done to avert it. And yet this seems to be precisely Yeats's point: the Apocalypse cannot be averted. It will be entirely unexpected, and we may not even be able to distinguish between our world's Savior and its Destroyer. In an age fascinated by post-apocalyptic dystopias, however, we believe we know what the Apocalypse will look like. We expect the anarchy, the blood-dimmed tides. Moreover, optimists believe that with enough foresight and determination, a sliver of humanity can survive whatever Armageddon has to throw at us. However, an end is hardwired into the fabric of Creation, and there is no way to prepare for it. Yeats's poem elicits discomfort because we are forced to come to terms with the fragile impermanence of our routine lives. These patterns will fall apart long before the End Times, as climate change, automation, or any number of unforeseen changes will cause the centres around which we have built our lives to fall apart. While Revelation might promise a heavenly new world, "The Second Coming" challenges us to first grapple with the uncomfortable prospect that the world as we understand it right now will soon face utter annihilation.

In her conclusion, Rachel reinforces her claim: that the poem prepares readers for the inevitable uncertainties of the world's end.

Works Cited

"Apocalypse, *noun.*" *Merriam-Webster.com Dictionary*, Merriam-Webster, 2019, https://www.merriam-webster.com/dictionary/apocalypse.

The Bible. New Oxford Annotated Version, 4th ed., Oxford UP, 2010.

Deane, Paul D. "Metaphors of Center and Periphery in Yeats' *The Second Coming.*" *Journal of Pragmatics*, vol. 24, no. 6, Dec. 1995, pp. 627–42.

Yeats, William Butler. "The Second Coming." *Reading and Writing about Literature: A Portable Guide*, edited by Janet E. Gardner and Joanne Diaz, 5th ed., Bedford/St. Martin's, 2021, p. 11.

Rachel employs a variety of sources, including a dictionary, a scholarly bible, and a scholarly article.

CHAPTER 9

Literary Criticism and Literary Theory

Anytime you sit down to write about literature, or even to discuss a story, play, or poem with your classmates, you are acting as a literary critic. Literary criticism includes everything from a glowing review to a scathing attack, to a thoughtful and balanced interpretation. Criticism can be broken down into two broad categories: evaluative and interpretive. Evaluative criticism seeks to determine how accomplished a work is and what place it should hold in the evolving story of literary history. Book reviews are the most common form of evaluative criticism. Interpretive criticism comprises all writing that seeks to explain, analyze, clarify, or question the meaning and significance of literature. Although you may engage in a certain amount of evaluative criticism in your literature class, and while your attitude about the value of literature will likely be apparent in your writing, the criticism you write for class will consist largely of interpretation.

All literary critics, including you, begin with some form of literary theory. Just as you may not have thought of yourself as a literary critic, you probably haven't thought of yourself as using literary theory. But you are doing so every time you write about literature, and it is a good idea to become familiar with some of the most prevalent types of theory. This familiarity will help you understand why so many respected literary critics seem to disagree with one another and why they write such different analyses of the same work of literature. It may also help to explain why you might disagree with your classmates, or even your instructor, in your interpretation of a particular story, poem, or play. Perhaps you are simply starting from a different theoretical base. You will be able to explain your thinking more eloquently if you understand that base.

Literary theory has the reputation of being incredibly dense and difficult. Indeed, the theories—sometimes called *schools* of criticism—discussed in the following pages are all complex, but here they are presented in their most basic, stripped-down forms. As such, these explanations are necessarily incomplete and selective. You should not feel you need to master the complexities of literary theory right now. You need only be aware of the existence of these various schools and watch for them as you read and write. Doing so will give you a better sense of what you're reading and hearing about the literature you explore, and it will make your writing more informed and articulate. There are many other schools and subschools in addition to those described here, but these are the most significant—the ones you are most likely to encounter as you continue to explore literature.

Focusing on Jamaica Kincaid's "Girl," T. S. Eliot's "The Love Song of J. Alfred Prufrock" (p. 112), and other works, the last paragraph of each entry offers a few directions one might take in a critical reading, with the specific critical theory applied to the analysis. While these notes are by no means exhaustive, they might help spark ideas for a paper, or at least grant greater insight into the literature and theory discussed.

FORMALISM AND NEW CRITICISM

For a large part of the twentieth century, literary criticism was dominated by various types of theory that can broadly be defined as *Formalism* and *New Criticism*. (New Criticism is no longer new, however, having begun to fall out of prominence in the 1970s, but its name lives on.) Formalist critics focus their attention on the formal elements of a literary text—things like **structure**, **tone**, **characters**, **setting**, **symbols**, and linguistic features. Explication and close reading (explained on pages 66–68) are techniques of Formalist criticism. While poetry, which is quite self-consciously formal in its structure, lends itself most obviously to Formalist types of criticism, prose fiction and drama are also frequently viewed through this lens.

Perhaps the most distinguishing feature of Formalism and New Criticism is that they focus on the text itself and not on extratextual factors. Formalist critics are interested in how parts of a text relate to one another and to the whole, and they seek to create meaning by unfolding and examining these relationships. Excluded from consideration are questions about the author, the reader, history or culture, and the relationship of the literary text to other texts or artwork. Chances are you have written some Formalist criticism yourself, either in high school or in college. If you have ever written a paper on **symbolism**, character development, or the relationship between sound patterns and sense in a poem, you have been a Formalist critic.

A Formalist critic of Jamaica Kincaid's story "Girl" might choose to focus on how the language used by the speaker of this monologue illuminates her character, while a Formalist critic of T. S. Eliot's "The Love Song of J. Alfred Prufrock" might focus on Eliot's irregular use of rhyme and meter in the poem.

FEMINIST AND GENDER CRITICISM

Have you ever had a classroom discussion of a piece of literature in which the focus was on the roles of women in the literature or the culture, or on the relationships between men and women? If so, you have engaged in **feminist criticism**. Some version of feminist criticism has been around for as long as readers have been interested in gender roles, but the school rose to prominence in the 1970s at the same time the modern feminist movement was gaining steam. Most feminist criticism from this time was clearly tied to raising consciousness about the patriarchy in which many women felt trapped. Some feminist critics sought to reveal how literary texts demonstrated the repression and powerlessness of women in different periods and cultures. Others had a nearly opposite agenda, showing how female literary characters could overcome the sexist power structures that surround them and exercise power in their worlds. Still, others looked to literary history and sought to rediscover and promote writing by women whose works had been far less likely than men's to be regarded as "great" literature.

Before long, however, some critics began to point out that women were not alone in feeling social pressure to conform to gender roles. Over the years, men have usually been expected to be good providers, to be strong (both physically and emotionally), and to keep their problems and feelings more or less to themselves. Though the expectations are different, men are socialized no less than women to think and behave in certain ways, and these social expectations are also displayed in works of literature. Feminist criticism has expanded in recent years to become **gender criticism**. Any literary criticism that highlights gender roles or relationships between the sexes can be a type of gender criticism, whether or not it is driven by an overt feminist agenda.

The story "Girl" would be an obvious choice for a feminist critic, since it focuses on how a young girl is socialized into the domestic roles expected of women in her society. A gender critic might also be interested in "Prufrock" and in the ways that the poem's aging speaker feels his masculinity called into question.

QUEER THEORY

Queer theory is one of the more recent critical schools to emerge out of critical interest in gender. It came into prominence in the 1990s, when some gay and lesbian literary critics perceived a need for a critical school that reflected their own particular circumstances and viewpoints. Some queer theorists insist that sexuality—or even the binary male/female division of gender itself—is culturally constructed rather than determined by physical characteristics present at birth. Many of these critics and theorists seek to destabilize the cultural norm that suggests that certain sexual preferences, marriage and family customs, and so forth are "normal" or "natural," while others are "deviant."

Queer theorists, like all literary critics, differ substantially in their focus. Some are interested in studying literary texts written by authors known to be members of the LGBTQIA+ community, particularly if these authors have been devalued in the past because of their sexual identity. Other queer theorists are interested in portrayals of LGBTQIA+ characters in literature written by all authors, regardless of their identification. Still others seek a "queer subtext" in canonical works of literature that have long been considered hetero-normative. (Included in this latter category are the many critics who have asked whether Shakespeare's Hamlet had something more than a traditional heterosexual friendship with his close confidant Horatio.)

At first glance, Jamaica Kincaid's "Girl" might not look like a promising candidate for examination by queer theory. But a queer theorist might, in fact, be interested in how the very possibility of homosexuality is erased by the narrator, the way the young girl is assumed to have an interest in "wharf-rat boys" and a need to know "how to love a man," though she never expresses these heterosexual urges.

MARXIST CRITICISM

Just as feminist criticism and queer theory came into their own because of broad political shifts in the culture, so, too, did **Marxist criticism**, which originally sought to use literature and criticism to forward a socialist political program. Early Marxist critics began with Karl Marx's (1818–1883) insistence that human interactions are economically driven and that the basic model of human progress is based on a struggle for power between different social classes. For Marxist critics, then, literature was just another battleground, another venue for the ongoing quest for individual material gain. Literary characters could be divided into powerful oppressors and their powerless victims, and literary plots and themes could be examined to uncover the economic forces that drove them. According to this model, the very acts of writing and reading literature can be characterized as production and consumption, and some Marxist critics have studied the external forces that drive education, publication, and literary tastes.

You no longer have to be a committed Marxist to engage in Marxist criticism; all you need to do is acknowledge that socioeconomic forces do, in fact, affect people's lives. If you notice inequalities in power between characters in a work of literature, if you question how the class or educational background of an author affects his or her work, or if you believe that a certain type of literature—a Shakespearean sonnet, say, or a pulp western novel—appeals more to readers of a particular social background, then you are, at least in part, engaging in Marxist criticism.

Social class roles, one of the primary interests of Marxist critics, are visible in the apparently modest circumstances of the characters in "Girl" (where class and gender have a clear overlap) as well as in the more bourgeois world of porcelain teacups and perfumed dresses on display in "Prufrock."

CULTURAL STUDIES

Cultural studies is the general name given to a wide variety of critical practices, some of which might seem on the surface to have little in common with one another. Perhaps the best way to understand cultural studies is to begin with the notion that certain texts are privileged in our society while others are dismissed or derided. Privileged texts are the so-called great works of literature commonly found in anthologies and on course syllabi. Indeed, when we hear the word *literature*, these are probably the works we imagine. All other writing—from pulp romance novels to the slogans on bumper stickers—belongs to a second category of texts, those generally overlooked by traditional literary critics.

One major trend in cultural studies is the attempt to broaden the **canon**—those texts read and taught again and again and held up as examples of the finest expressions of the human experience. Critics have pointed out that canonical authors—Shakespeare, Milton, Keats, Steinbeck—tend (with obvious exceptions) to be from a fairly narrow segment of society: they are usually middle- to upper-middle-class, well-educated, heterosexual white males. Some cultural critics, therefore, have sought out and celebrated the writing of historically disadvantaged groups such as African Americans or gay and lesbian authors. Other proponents of cultural studies turn their attention to the works of various social "outsiders," like prisoners, schoolchildren, or mental patients. This attempt at broadening the canon is designed to provide students and scholars alike with a more inclusive definition of what art and literature are all about.

Cultural critics seek to blur or erase the line separating "high" art from "low" art in the minds of the literary establishment. Some cultural critics believe that all texts are to some extent artistic expressions of a culture and that any text can therefore give us vital insights into the human experience. Rather than traditional literary objects, then, a cultural critic might choose to study such things as movies and television shows, advertisements, religious tracts, graffiti, and comic books. These texts—and virtually any other visual or verbal works you can imagine— are submitted to the same rigorous scrutiny as a sonnet or a classic novel. Some cultural critics suggest that English departments should become departments of cultural studies, in which a course on hip-hop culture would be valued as much as a course on Victorian poetry.

The poems of T. S. Eliot, including "The Love Song of J. Alfred Prufrock," occupy an important place in the early twentieth-century literary canon. A cultural critic might seek to explain how and why Eliot came to be so firmly associated with high culture.

POSTCOLONIAL CRITICISM

One very active branch of cultural studies is **postcolonial criticism**, which focuses on writing from former British (and other, mostly European) colonies around the world. Postcolonial criticism is most strongly associated with the Indian subcontinent (India, Pakistan, and Bangladesh), large portions of Africa and the Middle East, parts of Asia (such as Singapore and Vietnam), the Caribbean, and Latin America. In such places, indigenous authors often possess attitudes, tastes, and literary traditions very different from those of their former colonial masters. Postcolonial criticism seeks to discover these attitudes and tastes, to recover literary history that was ignored or suppressed during the colonial period, and to celebrate indigenous cultures of storytelling, drama, and poetry. At the same time, it attempts to understand how occupation by a more powerful colonizing nation disrupted and changed the course of history in a particular place.

In a colonial setting, members of the ruling group tend to see as natural and ordinary attitudes that might be better understood as racist, classist, and/or religiously intolerant, such as assuming that indigenous traditions are "superstitious" or "primitive" compared to the more "civilized" culture of the imperialists. Postcolonial theorists demand that indigenous attitudes and customs be treated with full respect and understanding. Postcolonial literary theory is situated within a larger move to comprehend the effect of colonial culture on history, art, architecture, politics, law, philosophy, sociology, sex and race relations, and daily life.

A postcolonial critic reading "Girl" would likely focus his or her attention on the details of language and culture—*benna* music, for instance, or the belief that blackbirds might really be spirits—that indicate that the story is in a particular postcolonial Caribbean setting.

HISTORICAL CRITICISM AND NEW HISTORICISM

If you have ever written a research paper that involved some background reading about the life and times of an author, you have already engaged in a form of **historical criticism**. Literary scholars have long read history books and various sorts of historical documents—from newspaper articles to personal letters—to gain insights into the composition and significance of a given work. The explanatory footnotes that often appear in literary reprints and anthologies are one obvious manifestation of this type of sleuthing. Indeed, some works of literature would be virtually inexplicable if we did not understand something of the times in which they were written and first read. If you did not know that Walt Whitman's "When Lilacs Last in the Dooryard Bloom'd" was an elegy written upon the assassination of Abraham Lincoln, it would be difficult to make any sense at all of the poem, since neither the president's name nor the cause of his death actually appear in the poem.

Likewise, historians have long turned to literary works and the visual arts in order to gain insights into the periods they study. While archives and contemporary documents can teach us a lot about the broad sweep of history—wars, leaders, the controversies of the day—it is often difficult to see from these documents what life was like for ordinary people, whose interior lives were not often documented. We may be able to learn from parish burial records, for example, how common childhood mortality was at a particular time in English history, but only when we read Ben Jonson's poem "On My First Son" (p. 18) do we begin to understand how this mortality may have affected the parents who lost their children. Likewise, the few pages of James Joyce's story "Araby" may tell us more about how adolescent boys lived and thought in early twentieth-century Dublin than would several volumes of social history.

One school of historical criticism, known as **New Historicism**, takes account of both what history has to teach us about literature *and* what literature has to teach us about history. (New Historicism has been around since the 1960s, and as with New Criticism, the name of the school is no longer as accurate as it once was.) New Historicists are sometimes said to read literary and nonliterary texts *in parallel*, attempting to see how each illuminates the other. Typically, New Historicists examine many different types of documents—government records, periodicals, private diaries, bills of sale—in order to re-create, as much as possible, the rich cultural context that surrounded both an author and that author's original audience. In doing so, they seek to give modern audiences a reading experience as rich and informed as the original readers of a literary work.

A historical critic of "Prufrock" might be able to untangle the meaning of certain lines or images that have little meaning for contemporary readers. These would include, for instance, what Prufrock means when he describes his "necktie rich and modest, but asserted by a simple pin" (line 43) or says, "I shall wear the bottoms of my trousers rolled" (121).

PSYCHOLOGICAL THEORIES

Early in the twenty-first century, it is easy to underestimate the enormous influence that the theories of the psychoanalyst Sigmund Freud (1856–1939) have had on our understanding of human behavior and motivation. For many modern readers, Freud seems to have little to say; his work is too focused on sex and too thoroughly bound by the norms of the bourgeois Viennese society in which he lived. But if you have ever wondered what the buried significance of a dream was or whether someone had a subconscious motivation for an action, you have been affected by Freudian thinking. Freud popularized the notions that the mind can be divided into conscious and unconscious components and that we are often motivated most strongly by the unconscious. He taught us to think in terms of overt and covert desires (often referred to in Freudian language as the words *manifest* and *latent*) as the basis of human actions.

Like many intellectual movements of the twentieth century, psychology, and specifically Freudian psychology, has had a major influence on literary criticism. The most typical **psychoanalytic literary criticism** examines the internal mental states, the desires, and the motivations of literary characters. (In fact, Freud himself used Shakespeare's Hamlet as an example of a man whose life was ruled by what the psychoanalyst called an Oedipal complex—man's unhealthy, but not uncommon, interest in his mother's sexuality.) Another subject of psychological criticism can be the author. A critic may examine the possible unconscious urges that drove an author to write a particular story or poem. Finally, a critic might examine the psychology of readers, trying to determine what draws us to or repels us from certain literary themes or forms. If any of these aspects of literature have ever interested you, you have engaged in psychoanalytic literary criticism.

Psychological critics often interpret literature as a psychologist might interpret a dream or a wish. Special attention is often paid to symbols as the manifest representation of a deeper, less obvious meaning. Attention is also focused on the unstated motives and unconscious states of mind of characters, authors, or readers. Freud is not the only psychological theorist whose ideas are frequently used in literary analysis.

Other important figures include Carl Jung (1875–1961), who gave us the notion of the collective unconscious and the influence of **archetypes** on our thinking, and Jacques Lacan (1901–1981), who had a special interest in the unconscious and the nature of language. However, you don't need to be well versed in the intricacies of psychoanalytic theory in order to be interested in the inner workings of the human mind or the ways in which they manifest themselves in literature.

The narrator of "Prufrock" is an excellent candidate for psychological study, displaying many signs of social anxiety, depression, and other recognizable psychological conditions. Or a Jungian critic of this poem might focus on archetypal symbols such as the animalistic fog early in the poem or the mermaids that appear near the end.

READER-RESPONSE THEORIES

You no doubt have heard the old question: If a tree falls in the forest and nobody hears it, did the tree make a sound? Let us rephrase that question: If a book sits on a shelf and nobody reads it, is it still a book? If you use **reader-response criticism**, your answer to that question will be a resounding *no*. Of course, the book exists as a physical object, a sheaf of paper bound in a cover and printed with symbols. But, as reader-response critics say, as a work of art or a conduit for meaning, no text exists without a reader.

A text, according to the various theories of reader-response criticism, is not a container filled with meaning by its author but rather an interaction between an author and a reader, and it can never be complete unless readers bring to it their own unique insights. These insights come from a number of sources, including the reader's life experience, as well as his or her beliefs, values, state of mind at the time of the reading, and, of course, previous reading experience. Reading is not a passive attempt to understand what lies within a text but an act of creation, no less so than the writing itself. Reader-response critics try to understand the process by which we make meaning out of words on a page. If you have ever wondered why a classmate or friend saw something entirely different than you did in a story or poem, then you have been a reader-response critic.

Two key terms associated with reader-response criticism are *gaps* and *process*. Gaps are those things that a text doesn't tell us, that we need to fill in and work out for ourselves. Let us say, for instance, that you read a story told from the perspective of a child, but the author never explicitly mentions the child's age. How, then, do you imagine the narrator as you read? You pay attention to his or her actions and thoughts, and you compare this to your experience of real children you have known and others whose stories you have read. In doing so, you fill in a *gap* in the text and help solidify the text's meaning. Imagine, though, that as the story continues, new clues emerge and you need to adjust your assumptions about the child's age. This highlights the idea that reading is a *process*, that the meaning of the text is not fixed and complete but rather evolving as the text unfolds in the time it takes to read.

Some reader-response critics focus on the ways that meanings of a text change over time. To illustrate this idea, let us look at a specific example. Contemporary readers of Kate Chopin's short novel *The Awakening*, first published in 1899, tend to find the book's treatment of the heroine's sexuality subtle or even invisible. Such readers are often shocked or amused to learn that the book was widely condemned at the time of its publication as tasteless and overly explicit. Expectations and tastes change over time and place, and we can tell a lot about a society by examining how it responds to works of art. Reader-response critics, therefore, sometimes ask us to look at our own reactions to literature and to ask how, if at all, they match up with those of earlier readers. When we look at reactions to *The Awakening* at the end of the nineteenth century and then at the beginning of the twenty-first century, we learn not only about Chopin's culture but also about our own.

STRUCTURALISM

Structuralism, as the name implies, is concerned with the structures that help us understand and interpret literary texts. This may sound like a return to Formalism, which, as we saw earlier, examines the formal and linguistic elements of a text. But the elements scrutinized by structuralist critics are of a different order entirely—namely, the structures that order our thinking rather than the interior architecture of poems, stories, and plays. Structuralist criticism actually derives from the work of anthropologists, linguists, and philosophers of the mid-twentieth century who sought to understand how humans think and communicate. The basic insight at the heart of the movement is the realization that we understand nothing in isolation but rather that every piece of our knowledge is part of a network of associations. Take, for instance, the question "Is Jim a good father?" In order to form a simple yes or no answer to this question, we must consider, among other things, the spectrum of "good" and "bad," the expectations our culture holds for fathers, and all we know of Jim's relationship with his children.

For a structuralist literary critic, questions about literature are answered with the same sort of attention to context. Two different types of context are especially salient—the cultural and the literary. Cultural context refers to an understanding of all aspects of an author's (and a reader's) culture, such as the organizing structures of history, politics, religion, education, work, and family. Literary context refers to all related texts, literary and nonliterary, that affect our ability to interpret a text. What had the author read that might have affected the creation of the text? What have we read that might affect our interpretation? What are the norms of the textual genre, and how does this piece of literature conform to or break from those norms?

According to structuralist critics, then, we can understand a text only by placing it within the broader contexts of culture (that of both the reader and the author) and other texts (literary and nonliterary). To fully understand one of Shakespeare's love sonnets to the mysterious "dark lady," for example, we would need to understand the conventions of romantic love, the conceptions of dark versus fair women in culturally accepted standards of beauty, and the acceptable interactions between men and women in Shakespeare's England. We would also need to relate the sonnet to the history of love poems generally, to the development of the sonnet form specifically, and to the other works in Shakespeare's cycle of 154 sonnets.

A structuralist reading of "Prufrock," then, would be likely to consider, among other things, the types of poetry that were in vogue in 1915, when the poem was first published, as well as the specific poems and poets that Eliot, who wrote literary criticism as well as poetry, most admired.

POSTSTRUCTURALISM AND DECONSTRUCTION

Poststructuralism, it will come as no surprise, begins with the insights of structuralism but carries them one step further. If, as the structuralists insist, we can understand things only in terms of other things, then perhaps there is no center point of understanding but only an endlessly interconnected web of ideas leading to other ideas leading to still other ideas. This is the starting point of poststructuralist criticism, which posits that no text has a fixed or real meaning because no meaning exists outside the network of other meanings to which it is connected. Meaning, then, including literary meaning, is forever shifting and altering as our understanding of the world changes. The best-known version of poststructuralism is **deconstruction**, a school of philosophy and literary criticism that first gained prominence in France and that seeks to overturn the very basis of Western philosophy by undermining the notion that reality has any stable existence.

At its worst, of course, this school of thought leads to the most slippery sort of relativism. What does it matter what I think of this poem or this play? I think what I want; you think what you want. Perhaps next week I will think something different. Who cares? Every interpretation is of equal value, and none has any real value at all. At its best, though, poststructuralist criticism can lead toward truly valuable insights into literature. It reminds us that meaning within a text is contingent on all sorts of exterior understandings; it allows for several interpretations, even contradictory interpretations, to exist simultaneously; and, by insisting that no text and no meaning are absolute, it allows for a playful approach to even the most "serious" of literary objects. Indeed, one of the recurrent themes of deconstructionist criticism is the French term *jouissance*, often translated as *bliss*, which refers to a free-spirited, almost-sexual enjoyment of literary language.

Having thus briefly described deconstruction, we would do well to dispel a common misconception about the word. In recent years, many people, both within and outside academia, have begun to use the word *deconstruct* as a synonym for *analyze*. You might hear, for instance, "We completely deconstructed that poem in class—I understand it much better now," or "The defense attorney deconstructed the prosecutor's argument." In both these cases, what the speaker likely means has little if anything to do with the literary critical practice of deconstruction. When we take apart a text or an argument and closely examine the parts, we are engaging not in deconstruction but in analysis.

A deconstructionist reading of "Girl" might call into question the very basis for our belief in gender divisions, class structure, or the need for the socialization of young people by their elders.

ECOCRITICISM

For much of human history, readers and writers have focused on the environment as it relates to human experience. Quite often, writers have largely treated the environment as a backdrop against which human action unfolds or as a force to be conquered, tamed, and exploited for its resources. Ecocriticism seeks to radically challenge that paradigm by asking a simple question: what would happen to literature—and its interpretation—if we were to reconsider, and perhaps foreground, nature and the environment as our primary site of interest? Ecocriticism is a necessarily interdisciplinary form of criticism. It draws from the fields of environmental studies, biology, philosophy, and natural history in order to investigate human interactions with nature. It is a broad mode of inquiry that has absorbed a number of theoretical frameworks, including feminist criticism, cultural studies, race theory, postcolonial studies, and Marxist criticism.

Ecocriticism can provide useful readings of nature writing. For example, how might an ecocritical reading of Henry David Thoreau's *Walden* provide readers with an understanding of how Thoreau drew upon motifs of American exceptionalism in his treatment of the landscape of the Concord and Merrimack Rivers? How might an ecocritical reading of William Wordsworth's "Tintern Abbey" allow readers to consider walking in nature as a valuable form of self-discovery? Ecocriticism can also be used for texts that are several thousand years old, such as the Book of Genesis from the Hebrew Bible. For example, how do the creation stories in Genesis lay a foundation for a human-centered universe that many people rely on to this day? Ecocriticism can be very valuable when reading more recent work by contemporary poets such as Mary Oliver, Juliana Spahr, and Ross Gay, as well. For example, how might a poem reveal the intersections between race and the environment in new and compelling ways?

In recent years, ecocritics have become particularly interested in the era referred to as the Anthropocene—that period during which human activity has directly affected the environment. Some scientists and historians point to the Industrial Revolution as the beginning of the Anthropocene era, while others push even further into the past, suggesting that European colonization in the sixteenth century marked the beginning of the Anthropocene. In recent years, ecocriticism has sought to investigate how industrialization, technology, and the forces of capitalism have affected how we tell our stories, and how our stories will necessarily be influenced by the inevitability of climate change.

These are only some of the many varieties of literary theory and criticism. In addition, you might encounter religious (for example, Christian, Muslim, or Buddhist) criticism; comparative literature, which compares related works from different languages and/or cultures; various schools of critical inquiry based on race and ethnicity; and many, many more. There are even literary critics who perform textual analysis using sophisticated computer programs.

By now you may be wondering what sort of literary critic you are. You may feel that you have been a Formalist one day and a psychological critic the next. This is not surprising, and it should cause you no worry; none of these schools are mutually exclusive. Indeed, most professional critics mix and match the various schools in whatever way best suits their immediate needs. The close-reading techniques of the New Critics, for instance, are frequently adopted by those who would fervently reject the New Critical stance that social and political context be excluded from consideration. If you wished to write about the social decline of Mme. Loisel in Guy de Maupassant's story "The Necklace," you might well find yourself in the position of a Marxist–feminist–New Historicist critic. That's fine. Writing with the knowledge that you are drawing from Marxism, feminism, and New Historicism, you will almost certainly write a better-organized, better-informed, and more thorough paper than you would have had you begun with no conscious basis in literary theory.

Take a look at the annotations and notes you have made on literary works, the notes you have taken in class, and any exams or papers you have written. Are there particular themes and issues to which you keep returning, particular genres or literary features that continue to attract or interest you? If so, you may have the beginning of an answer to the question: *What sort of literary critic am I?*

Glossary of Critical and Literary Terms

This glossary provides definitions for important literary terms used in this anthology. Words and phrases highlighted in **boldface** in individual entries are defined elsewhere in the glossary.

Accentual-syllabic verse Verse whose meter takes into account both the number of syllables per line and the pattern of accented and unaccented syllables. The great majority of metrical poems in English are accentual-syllabic.

Antagonist The character (or, less often, the force) that opposes the **protagonist**.

Archetype An image, symbol, character type, or plot line that occurs frequently enough in literature, religion, myths, folktales, and fairy tales to be recognizable as an element of universal experience and that evokes a deep emotional response.

Assonance The repetition of identical or similar vowel sounds in words relatively near to one another (usually within a line or in adjacent lines) whose consonant sounds differ.

Ballad A poem that tells a story and was meant to be recited or sung; originally, a folk art transmitted orally, from person to person and from generation to generation. Many of the popular ballads were not written down and published until the eighteenth century, though their origins may have been centuries earlier.

Caesura A pause or break within a line of verse, usually signaled by a mark of punctuation.

Canon The group of literary works that form the backbone of a cultural tradition.

Characters, characterization Broadly speaking, characters are usually the people of a work of literature—although characters may be animals or some other beings. In fiction, characterization means the development of a character or characters throughout a story. Characterization includes the narrator's description of what characters look like and what they think, say, and do (these are sometimes very dissimilar). Their own actions and views of themselves, and other characters' views of and behavior toward them, are also means of characterization. Characters may be minor, like Goody Cloyse, or major, like Goodman Brown, both of Hawthorne's "Young Goodman Brown". Depending on the depth of characterization, a character may be simple or complex, flat or round. Character is one of the six **elements of drama** identified by Aristotle, and characterization is the process by which writers and actors make a character distinct and believable to an audience.

Consonance   The repetition of consonant sounds in words whose vowels are different. In perfect consonance, all consonants are the same—*live, love*; *chitter, chatter*; *reader, rider*; words in which all consonants following the main vowels are identical also are considered consonant—*dive, love*; *swatter, chitter*; *sound, bond*; *gate, mat*; *set, pit*.

Cultural context   The milieu that gives rise to a work of literature.

Cultural studies   A general name given to a wide variety of critical practices that examine and challenge why certain texts are privileged in our society while others are dismissed or derided. Rather than focusing on traditional literary objects, cultural studies critics might choose to study movies, television shows, advertisements, graffiti, or comic books, often in conjunction with **canonical** works of literature.

Deconstruction   A variety of **poststructuralism**, deconstruction derives from the efforts of Jacques Derrida to undermine the foundations of Western philosophy, but as a literary critical practice it often emerges as a kind of close-reading that reveals irreconcilable linguistic contradictions in a text that prevents it from having a single stable meaning or message.

Dialogue   Words spoken by characters, often in the form of a conversation between two or more characters. In stories and other forms of prose, dialogue is commonly enclosed between quotation marks. Dialogue is an important element in **characterization** and **plot**: much of the characterization and action in Ernest Hemingway's "Hills Like White Elephants" is presented through its characters' dialogue.

Diction   A writer's selection of words; the kind of words, phrases, and figurative language used to make up a work of literature. In fiction, particular patterns or arrangements of words in sentences and paragraphs constitute prose style. Hemingway's diction is said to be precise, concrete, and economical. Aristotle identified diction as one of the six **elements of drama**. See also **poetic diction**.

Dramatic monologue   A poem with only one speaker, overheard in a dramatic moment (usually addressing another character or characters who do not speak), whose words reveal what is going on in the scene and expose significant depths of the speaker's temperament, attitudes, and values. See Robert Browning's "My Last Duchess" (p. 69) and T. S. Eliot's "The Love Song of J. Alfred Prufrock" (p. 112).

Elements of drama   The six features identified by Aristotle in *Poetics* as descriptive of and necessary to drama. They are, in order of the importance assigned to them by Aristotle, **plot**, **characterization**, **theme**, **diction**, **melody**, and **spectacle**.

Elements of fiction   Major elements of fiction are **plot**, **characters**, **setting**, **point of view**, **style**, and **theme**. Skillful employment of these entities is essential in effective novels and stories. From beginning to end, each element is active and relates to the others dynamically.

End-stopped line   A line of poetry whose grammatical structure and thought reach completion by its end. Cf. **run-on line**.

Enjambment   See **run-on line**.

Epic   A long narrative poem that celebrates the achievements of great heroes and heroines, often determining the fate of a tribe or nation, written in formal language and an elevated style. Examples include Homer's *Iliad* and *Odyssey*, Virgil's *Aeneid*, and John Milton's *Paradise Lost*.

Explication   The process of making clear that which is implicit or subtle in a work of literature. This is achieved by performing a close-reading—reading a piece of literature with an eye toward such sentence-level elements as sentence structure, style, imagery, word choice, and figurative language—and then explaining the larger purpose and effect of those elements.

Feminist criticism   A school of literary criticism that examines the roles of women in literature and culture as well as the relationships between men and women. Contemporary feminist criticism rose to prominence in the 1970s, when the modern feminist movement began to explore the patriarchal structures in which many women felt trapped. Some feminist critics seek to show the ways in which literary texts demonstrate the repression and powerlessness of women—or, alternately, to show how female literary characters could overcome sexist power structures. Still others seek to rediscover and promote writing by women whose works have been excluded from the mostly male **canon** of "great" literature.

First-person narrator   In a story told by one person, the *I* who tells the story. Sometimes the first-person narrator is purely an observer; more often he or she is directly or indirectly involved in the action of the story. Montresor is the first-person narrator of, and one of two characters in, Edgar Allan Poe's "The Cask of Amontillado". As a first-person narrator, he reveals much about his own emotions and motivations.

Free verse   See **open form**.

Gender criticism   A broad term for literary criticism that highlights gender roles or relationships between the sexes. In this expansive sense, **feminist criticism** is a kind of gender criticism, although the latter term is most often applied to gay and lesbian approaches to literature that explore the construction of sexual identity.

Genre   A type or form of literature. While the major literary genres are **fiction**, **drama**, **poetry**, and exposition, many other subcategories of genres are recognized, including **comedy**, **tragedy**, **tragicomedy**, **romance**, **melodrama**, **epic**, **lyric**, **pastoral**, **novel**, **short story**, and so on.

Historical criticism   A kind of literary criticism based on the notion that history and literature are often interrelated. For example, literary critics might read history books and various sorts of historical documents in order to gain insights into the composition and significance of a literary work.

Image   (1) Sometimes called a "word-picture," an image is a word or group of words that refers to a sensory experience or to an object that can be known by one or more of the senses. **Imagery** signifies all such language in a poem or other literary work collectively and can involve any of the senses. See also **synesthesia**. (2) A metaphor or other comparison. **Imagery** in this sense refers to the characteristic that several images in a poem may have in common, as for example, the Christian imagery in William Blake's "The Lamb".

Juxtaposition The placement of things side by side or close together for comparison or contrast, or to create something new from the union.

Lineation The arrangement of lines in a poem.

Lyric Originally, a poem sung to the accompaniment of a lyre; now a short poem expressing the personal emotion and ideas of a single speaker.

Marxist criticism Deriving from Karl Marx's theories of economics and class struggle, Marxist criticism sees literature as a material product of work, one that reflects or contests the ideologies that generated its production and consumption.

Motivation What drives a character to act in a particular way. To be convincing to an audience, an actor must understand and make clear to the audience the character's motivation.

Narrative A story in prose or verse; an account of events involving characters and a sequence of events told by a storyteller (narrator). A poem such as Naomi Shihab Nye's "Gate A-4" tells a story and is thus a **narrative poem**. Usually, the characters can be analyzed and generally understood; the events unfold in a cause-and-effect sequence; and some unity can be found among the characters, plot, point of view, style, and theme. Novels as well as stories are most often narratives, and journalism commonly employs narrative form.

Narrative poem See **narrative**.

New Criticism A kind of **formalism** that dominated Anglo-American literary criticism in the middle decades of the twentieth century. It emphasized close-reading, particularly of poetry, to discover how a work of literature functioned as a self-contained, self-referential aesthetic object.

New Historicism A school of **historical criticism** that takes account of both what history has to teach us about literature *and* what literature has to teach us about history. New Historicists examine many different types of texts—government records, periodicals, private diaries, bills of sale—in order to re-create, as much as possible, the rich cultural context that surrounded both an author and that author's original audience.

Omniscient narrator A narrator who seems to know everything about a story's events and characters, even their inner feelings. Usually, an omniscient narrator maintains emotional distance from the characters.

Open form A form free of any predetermined metrical and stanzaic patterns. Cf. **closed form**.

Paraphrase To restate a passage of literature or criticism in your own words, particularly useful as a method for taking research notes, or for interpreting a text. Generally, a paraphrase will be about equal in length to the passage being paraphrased, while a **summary** will be much shorter.

Plagiarism   The act of closely imitating or outright adopting the language or ideas of another author and presenting them as one's own work without giving credit to the original author. This includes copying and pasting from any Web source. Most colleges and universities have codes of academic honesty forbidding such practices and imposing severe penalties—including expulsion from the institution in some cases—on students who are caught breaking them.

Plot   (1) The sequence of major events in a story, usually related by cause and effect. **Plot development** refers to how the sequence evolves or is shaped. Plot and character are intimately related, since characters carry out the plot's action. Plots may be described as simple or complex, depending on their degree of complication. "Traditional" writers, such as Edgar Allan Poe, usually plot their stories tightly; modernist writers such as James Joyce employ looser, often ambiguous plots. (2) The action that takes place within the play. Of the six **elements of drama**, Aristotle considered plot to be the most important. Typical elements of plot include a **prologue** or **exposition**, **rising action**, **complication**, **climax**, **falling action**, and **catastrophe** or **denouement**.

Point of view   One of the elements of fiction, point of view is the perspective, or angle of vision, from which a narrator presents a story. Point of view tells us about the **narrator** as well as about the characters, setting, and theme of a story. Two common points of view are *first-person narration* and *third-person narration*. If a narrator speaks of himself or herself as *I*, the narration is in the first person; if the narrator's self is not apparent and the story is told about others from some distance, using *he*, *she*, *it*, and *they*, then third-person narration is likely in force. The point of view may be omniscient (all-knowing) or limited, objective or subjective. When determining a story's point of view, it is helpful to decide whether the narrator is reporting events as they are happening or as they happened in the past; is observing or participating in the action; and is or is not emotionally involved. Shirley Jackson's "The Lottery" is told from the third-person objective point of view, since its narrator observes what the character is doing, thinking, and feeling, yet seems emotionally distant. Edgar Allan Poe's "The Cask of Amontillado" is told in the first-person subjective and limited point of view, since its narrator is very much involved in the action. In Kate Chopin's "The Story of an Hour" (p. 99), shifting points of view enable us to see Mrs. Mallard from the outside, as her family does (third-person objective); learn about her most private emotional responses and secrets (third-person subjective); and hear her thoughts directly as if we were inside her mind (first-person subjective).

Postcolonial criticism   A branch of cultural studies that focuses on writing from former European colonies around the world. Postcolonial criticism seeks to recover literary history that was ignored or suppressed during the colonial period, and to celebrate indigenous cultures of storytelling, drama, and poetry. At the same time, it attempts to understand how occupation by a more powerful colonizing nation disrupted and changed the course of history in a particular place.

Poststructuralism A theory positing that no text can have a fixed or real meaning because no meaning can exist outside the network of other meanings to which it is connected. It carries the insights of **structuralism** one step further. If, as structuralists claim, we can understand things only in terms of other things, then perhaps there is no center point of understanding, but only an endlessly interconnected web of ideas leading to other ideas leading to still other ideas. Meaning, then, is forever shifting and altering as our understanding of the world changes.

Primary source Term used in writing about literature to refer to the literature itself—the poem, story, or play on which the writing is based. Cf. **secondary source**.

Protagonist The lead character of a play, though not necessarily a **hero** in the classic sense.

Psychoanalytic criticism A broad term for the various types of literary theory that focus on the inner workings of the human psyche and the ways in which they manifest themselves in literature. Psychoanalytic critics often interpret literature as a psychologist might interpret a dream or a wish, often paying special attention to unstated motives and to the unconscious states of mind in characters, authors, or readers.

Queer theory Queer theorists, like all literary critics, differ substantially in their focus: Some queer theorists are interested in studying literary texts written by authors known or suspected to be gay, lesbian, bisexual, or transgender. Other queer theorists are interested in portrayals of gay or lesbian characters in literature. Still others seek a queer subtext in canonical works of literature that have long been considered heteronormative.

Reader-response criticism The various theories of reader-response criticism hold that a text is an interaction between author and reader, and a text can never be complete unless readers bring to it their own unique insights. Reading, then, is not a passive attempt to understand a text but is itself an act of creation, no less than writing.

Rhyme The repetition of the accented vowel sound of a word and all succeeding consonant sounds. See also **exact rhyme**; **slant rhyme**.

Scansion The division of metrical verse into feet in order to determine and label its meter. Scanning a poem involves marking its stressed syllables with an accent mark (´) and its unstressed syllables with a curved line (˘), and using a vertical line to indicate the way a line divides into feet, then describing (or labeling) the type of foot used most often and the line length—that is, the number of feet in each line. See also **foot** and **line**.

Secondary source Outside source used in writing about literature: biographical, historical, or critical writing that discusses the literature but is not the literature itself. (The literature itself is considered a **primary source**.)

Set The stage dressing for a play, consisting of backdrops, furniture, and similar large items.

Setting One of the elements of fiction, setting is the context for the action: the time, place, culture, and atmosphere in which it occurs. A work may have several settings; the relation among them may be significant to the meaning of the work. In Nathaniel Hawthorne's "Young Goodman Brown", for example, the larger setting is seventeenth-century Puritan Salem, Massachusetts, but Brown's mysterious journey is set in a forest, and its prelude and melancholy aftermath are set in the village.

Short story   A short work of narrative fiction whose plot, characters, settings, point of view, style, and theme reinforce one another, often in subtle ways, creating an overall unity.

Slant rhyme   Consonance at the ends of lines; for example, *Room* and *Storm*, *firm* and *Room*, and *be* and *Fly* in Emily Dickinson's "I heard a Fly buzz — when I died". It can also be internal, if repeated enough to form a discernible pattern.

Sonnet   A fourteen-line poem usually written in **iambic pentameter**; originally lyrical love poems, sonnets came to be used also for meditations on religious themes, death, and nature and are now open to all subjects. Some variations in form have been tried: George Meredith wrote sixteen-line sonnets; and American poet Robert Hayden abandons fixed rhyme altogether in "Those Winter Sundays."

Speaker   The persona(e) voicing the poem. The speaker is sometimes the poet, though other times a poem may speak from a different perspective.

Stage directions   Written instructions in the script telling actors how to move on the stage or how to deliver a particular line. To facilitate the reading of scripts and to distinguish them from simple dialogue, stage directions are interspersed throughout the text, typically placed in parentheses and set in italics.

Stanza   A grouping of poetic lines into a section, either according to form — each section having the same number of lines and the same prosody — or according to thought, creating irregular units comparable to paragraphs in prose.

Structuralism   Structuralism is concerned with the cognitive and cultural structures that help us understand and interpret literary texts. The basic insight at the heart of the movement is the realization that we understand nothing in isolation, but rather that every piece of knowledge is part of a network of associations.

Structure   (1) The framework — the general plan, outline, or organizational pattern — of a literary work; (2) narrower patterns within the overall framework. Cf. **form.**

Style   One of the elements of fiction, style refers to the diction (choice of words), syntax (arrangement of words), and other linguistic features of a literary work. Just as no two people have identical fingerprints or voices, so no two writers use words in exactly the same way. Style distinguishes one writer's language from another's. William Faulkner and Ernest Hemingway, two major modern writers, had very different styles.

Summary   A brief recap of the most important points in a work of literature, such as plot, character, or setting.

Symbol   Something that is itself and also stands for something else; a literary symbol is a prominent or repeated image or action that is present in a story, poem, or play and can be seen, touched, smelled, heard, tasted, or experienced imaginatively, but also conveys a cluster of abstract meanings beyond itself. Most critics agree that the wallpaper in Charlotte Perkins Gilman's "The Yellow Wallpaper" (p. 85) and the tiger in William Blake's "The Tyger", for example, carry symbolic meaning. See also **archetype**.

Symbolism The use of objects or events to suggest meaning beyond their immediate, physical presence. Symbolism exists in all genres of literature, but in drama it might include visual or sound elements as well as language.

Text Traditionally, a piece of writing. In **reader-response criticism**, "text" has come to mean the words with which the reader interacts; in this view, a story, poem, or play is not an object, not a shape on the page or a spoken performance, but what is apprehended and completed in the reader's mind.

Theme The central idea embodied by or explored in a literary work; the general concept, explicit or implied, that the work incorporates and makes persuasive to the reader. Other literary elements, including characters, plot, settings, point of view, figurative language, symbols, and style, contribute to a theme's development.

Thesis statement A few sentences, usually located toward the beginning of a paper, declaring the position the author plans to take on the proposed topic.

Third-person narrator The type of narration being used if a storyteller is not identified, does not speak of himself or herself with the pronoun *I*, asserts no connection between the narrator and the characters in the story, and tells the story with some objectivity and distance, using the pronouns *he*, *she*, *it*, and *they* — but not *I*.

Tone The implied attitude, or "stance," toward the subject and toward the reader or audience in a literary work; the "tone of voice" it seems to project (serious or playful; exaggerated or understated; formal or informal; ironic or straightforward; or a complex mixture of more than one of these). For example, the tone of Toni Cade Bambara's "The Lesson" is streetwise and tough, the voice of its first-person narrator.

Tragedy A play in which the **plot** moves from relative stability to death or other serious sorrow for the **protagonist**. A traditional tragedy is written in a grand style and shows a **hero** of high social stature brought down by **peripeteia** or by events beyond his or her control.

Villanelle A nineteen-line lyric poem divided into five **tercets** and a final four-line stanza, rhyming *aba aba aba aba aba abaa*. Line 1 is repeated to form lines 6, 12, and 18; line 3 is repeated to form lines 9, 15, and 19.

Acknowledgments (Continued from page iv)
Editors of *Encyclopædia Britannica*, excerpt from "William Butler Yeats." Copyright © 2019 by Encyclopædia Britannica, Inc. Reprinted with permission from Encyclopædia Britannica.

Index